THE PLAY-READER'S HANDBOOK

ROBERT F. WHITMAN

University of Pittsburgh

THE PLAY-READER'S HANDBOOK

PN
1657
W45

The Bobbs-Merrill Company, Inc.
A SUBSIDIARY OF HOWARD W. SAMS & CO., INC.
Publishers   INDIANAPOLIS · NEW YORK · KANSAS CITY

CONTENTS

INTRODUCTION

Only the twentieth century could produce a handbook on how to read a play. In any age but our own, such a book would have been viewed with amazement, much as a pamphlet called "How to Listen to Popular Music" or "How to Watch Television" would be today. During most of the past two thousand years, plays have provided as natural and unself-conscious a form of entertainment as movies and television do now. Drama has been the most direct, the most immediately appealing of literary art forms, and as such it has generally reached a wider audience than has either fiction or poetry.

Why, then, a handbook on drama? Is the modern reader less well educated or less sophisticated than his counterparts in other centuries, that he needs to be told how to read plays? Not necessarily; the point is simply that he has been denied the opportunity to see them. In our own time, for better or worse, various economic and technical developments have served to make "legitimate" stage drama less and less familiar to the great majority of Americans.

Although many people have their theories, it is practically im-

viii   possible to isolate all the factors that have contributed to the decline of the drama in mid-twentieth-century America—a decline not necessarily in the quality of plays, but in the percentage of the population that attends them. The most obvious element here is the steadily increasing inroads made first by motion pictures and then by television on a potential theater-going audience. For some, this is simply proof that what they call bad art drives out good. But the economic factor cannot be overlooked. Obviously, movies and television offer less expensive and more accessible media of dramatic entertainment than the stage, and the professional theater, bedeviled by rising costs and a dwindling audience, can rarely succeed commercially outside such huge concentrations of humanity as New York City.

The problem is a complex one, and the circle is vicious in a more than purely economic sense. The smaller and more select the audience, the more "private" and esoteric plays tend to become and the larger the number of people who stay home to watch their television sets. The question of simple habit also enters in—a kind of reversal of the principle of "the more you eat, the more you want." People who are used to playgoing will create their own demand; but as fewer plays are produced, fewer people will take for granted the desirability of seeing them. Interest in drama in this country, as evidenced by amateur theatricals, was at its height when the road-show circuit was in its prime in the early decades of the twentieth century; but both are dead or dying. Little more than a melancholy sigh has been heard as what was once the liveliest of the arts has gradually retreated into the hothouse world of Broadway or the rather exclusive one of the universities.

This epitaph on the demise of legitimate theater is, of course, an oversimplification; there are certainly a fortunate few, living in communities with vital and active theaters, whether commercial or amateur, for whom seeing a play performed on the stage is a form of entertainment as "natural" as reading a short story or watching a television show. In spite of exceptions, however, the vast majority of Americans are caught in a vicious circle: On the one hand, only when they want to see plays will a theater grow up to produce them; and, on the other, only where there is a background of experience in the theater will the want exist.

Experience, or the lack of it, is in fact the clue to the whole problem. It is precisely because motion pictures are so familiar to us that they can be convincing and effective, and it is largely because Greek or Elizabethan or Restoration or even many modern dramas are not familiar to us that they may seem stiff, unreal, and "artistic." Motion pictures make much greater demands on our credulity than do most plays—but the demands are more familiar and the concessions therefore easier to make. An Elizabethan audience, for example, which saw nothing at all difficult or strange about Shakespeare's plays, would probably have found the movies, as a dramatic medium, thoroughly incomprehensible. And the reverse is generally true for us.

The ideal solution, of course, is for us to see plays, many plays, plays of our own century and of earlier ages, until we have built up a background of experience that will make each new dramatic encounter comprehensible and rewarding. But, as we have seen, this ideal is, practically speaking, unattainable for a large number of Americans. Their best alternative, it would seem, is reading plays.

The printed page and the theater obviously are not interchangeable media, but the experience of reading a play can in its own way be highly rewarding. Reading is particularly valuable when the play belongs to an unfamiliar tradition. Stage action and stage dialogue, as well as the conventions and illusions employed by the dramatist, can move by so rapidly that an inexperienced audience may miss them completely. Someone whose first contact with Shakespeare occurs in the theater may well find his plays unintelligible. Reading drama at least has the virtue of allowing us to slow the pace to match our ability to absorb, to read and reread passages or episodes until they make sense.

It is as a guide or short cut between inexperience and experience that this handbook is designed. The gap is not an easy one to fill, especially in the absence of actual dramatic productions,

Introduction

but with some help it can be bridged. The basic premise of the book is that, as has been suggested, modern failure to understand and enjoy drama is principally the result of unfamiliarity with what might be called the "language" of the theater—the methods a playwright uses to tell his story and the devices he employs to convince us that it is "real." It is scarcely necessary to point out that very little about a play is literally real, even when it is produced on a stage. The setting is not what *it* pretends to be, the actors are not what *they* pretend to be, the language is such as was never spoken by living man. It's all a fraud, from beginning to end; and unless the playwright can convince us that what he writes is true, that there is some valid point of contact between his characters and their world and their problems, and what we call reality, he will never find an audience.

All this is quite obvious; less obvious are the various ways in which a dramatist endows his little world of the stage with the ability to convince. It is a matter partly of his having roughly the same view of the world and of human nature as his audience, partly of his sharing with them a concept of what the theater and drama are, and partly of certain unspoken agreements between playwright and audience as to what will be accepted as "standing for" reality. Much more will be said of these requirements later; but they are representative of what must be understood before a play is really intelligible. The playwright, in other words, makes certain assumptions about the nature of reality and about the way in which reality can best and most truly be shadowed forth on a physical stage with human actors or in the imaginations of readers. The assumptions change from age to age and, in our own time at least, from playwright to playwright. The purpose of this handbook is to prepare the reader for experiencing many types of plays by suggesting what the relevant assumptions are.

The book does not, however, presume to do everything; much material that the serious student of drama will eventually want and need has not here been covered.[1] The history of the theater is a fascinating and rewarding study, as is the investigation of

[1] See the Bibliography, page 211.

the milieus—social, political, and cultural—in which various plays were written. But these topics deserve volumes in themselves; they are touched on here only to the extent that seems absolutely necessary to the understanding of a particular dramatic tradition. There are books that deal exhaustively with the structure of plays, or with aesthetic theories about drama, or with the principles and terminology of dramatic criticism. But, again, these matters are considered here only insofar as is necessary to provide the language and the concepts that we need in order to talk about plays at all. In other words, this handbook seeks to achieve its purpose with brevity and simplicity; it does not aim at comprehensiveness.

As to organization: The first half of the book moves from the known to the less well known. It starts with the assumption that motion pictures represent the only dramatic tradition with which everyone is familiar, and consequently it begins by pointing out various important analogies and differences between movies and the closest tradition in stage drama, contemporary realism. Then, since the principal differences among plays of various periods and types arise from the differing concepts of "reality" on which they are based, consideration is given to some of the ways in which modern "nonrealistic" playwrights deal with the real world. Finally, in the second portion of the book, the general conclusions arrived at in the first part are applied to plays of particular periods in the world's history when drama has been at its height. Without attempting a history of drama, the book concentrates in more or less chronological fashion on those assumptions about the nature of reality which appear in the drama of ancient Greece, Elizabethan England, Restoration England, nineteenth-century England and Europe, and contemporary Europe and America.

Most books of this nature include as part of their format an anthology of plays chosen to illustrate the points made in the text. Such selections can indeed be useful, especially when one desires to make a close analysis of a specific text. The trouble with anthologies is, however, that no one—teacher or student or reader for pastime—is ever quite satisfied with someone else's selections.

The solution seemed to be, then, to provide no anthology at all. Since virtually all major plays of the world are readily and cheaply available in paperback editions, I saw no point in imposing my tastes on others. From the plays used as examples in the text, and from the supplementary reading lists appended to each chapter, it is possible for the reader to make up a list of his own that adequately illuminates the discussion. While this method loses something in specificity, it gains much in flexibility, and it is my hope that it will make the book more pleasurable and more practical for those who use it.

R. F. W.

Pittsburgh, Pennsylvania
October 1965

Part One

The Nature and Kinds of "Reality" in Drama

Drama as Experience

What is drama? This is a simple and reasonable question, not so elementary as to be beneath our consideration; and certainly a handbook on drama might reasonably be expected to answer it. But men have been asking this simple question for about two thousand years and have failed to arrive at a really satisfactory answer. Perhaps because the query is so basic, it does not permit a straightforward answer. Or, to be paradoxical about it, the answer that is simple enough to be comprehensive is so vague as to be no help at all.

Aristotle was the first dramatic critic and, because he was a highly perceptive man working in an untouched field, he said many things that have not been improved upon in the twenty centuries since he wrote. Most discussions of what drama is, consequently, go back at some point to his descriptive statement in *The Poetics*. Although Aristotle deals only with tragedy, his comments may be taken to apply to drama in general. He says that "tragedy is an imitation of an action that is complete and whole and of a certain magnitude. . . . A whole is that which has a beginning, a middle, and an end."[1] This sounds rather impressive

[1] Aristotle, *On the Art of Poetry,* tr. S. H. Butcher, ed. Milton C. Nahm, "The Library of Liberal Arts," No. 6 (New York: The Liberal Arts Press, Inc., 1956), p. 11.

but a little enigmatic. What exactly does it mean? Later critics have filled many pages and even volumes amplifying Aristotle's statement, trying to make clear in many words what is by no means clear in a few. But as we try to pin down the rather nebulous terminology, to define it further and make it more explicit, we at the same time necessarily restrict and limit his meaning. Indeed it seems likely that Aristotle kept his language as general as possible precisely because he wanted to make his definitions as universal as possible.

Even so, the passage from *The Poetics* does offer some concrete help. Some of the distinctive features of drama, it suggests, are that it is an *imitation,* in the sense of an imaginative re-creation, rather than a narration or description; that what is imitated is not merely a character or an idea or a static picture, but an *action;* and that this action is of some magnitude (we might say significance). What is most striking about the passage, though, is its emphasis on unity. A play is *an* action; and, while it must have some complexity, it is seen as a related series of events forming a *whole* that is complete in itself and possesses a recognizable order ("a beginning, a middle, and an end").

This may seem fairly elementary, but it is important, and we will come back to it from time to time. We might well want our description of drama to take account of even more specific characteristics—for instance, that the imitation is intended to be carried out by actors on a stage. We must be careful, however, not to limit our terms too closely, since what is certainly drama has been performed in the nave of a church, in the streets, on an open plot of ground, in a movie studio. Perhaps we would like to include some attempt to characterize the content or subject matter of plays, and to say that only certain kinds of actions are appropriate for dramatic representation. But, over its long history, drama has employed such a variety of objects for "imitation" that almost no generalizations are safe. Drama has "imitated" actions both "real" and imaginary. The events represented have been of the external world and of the mind—the world of dreams and nightmares, or of the grotesque symbols of modern psychology.

The Nature and Kinds of "Reality" in Drama

The characters have been historical, supernatural, allegorical, or the product of the wildest fantasy. It would be risky to limit ourselves even to the extent of saying that the subject matter of drama must be specifically human. On the other hand, we *can* say that the action must be sufficiently relevant to human affairs, if only by analogy, to engage our interest and attention. It must somehow "speak" to us.

This suggests that the essence of drama may lie not only in its form, in *how* it is done, but in *what* it does—its effect. Aristotle recognizes this dimension of any attempt to define drama; to the description already quoted he adds the identifying feature of tragedy: that "through pity and fear it achieves the proper purgation (catharsis) of such emotions." But we must take as a kind of warning the fact that for several centuries critics have been arguing heatedly as to how we are to understand the terms *pity* and *fear* and what psychological process *purgation* is intended to describe. The trouble with any effort to talk about the effect of drama is that this effect is necessarily—at least in part—subjective and personal and, therefore, to a degree incommunicable.

The source of the difficulty is the fact that drama, along with other forms of literature and indeed all art, falls into a category of entities that are ultimately indefinable. Love, for instance, is impossible to define absolutely, because it is not an object or a predictable physical phenomenon; it is something that *happens* to someone. It is an experience and, as such, may perhaps be described but cannot be translated into terms that will define this category of experience for all people. We can say, "Love is a strong feeling of attraction for someone," but this is not only woefully inadequate, it is, as a statement, simply of a different order of "thing" from the experience itself. And in much the same way, drama is not merely an abstraction or the fulfillment of certain rules, nor can it be said really to exist until it is an experience.

One of the many advantages of treating drama as one kind of human experience (rather than as primarily a collection of functional elements called "setting," "plot," or "characterization," organized according to certain laws) is that this viewpoint provides the reader with a more satisfactory—or at least a more satisfying—basis for judging the value of particular plays. Many plays have been written that followed all the most widely accepted "rules" of play construction, yet have left their audiences totally unresponsive. On the other hand, probably almost as many plays have defied all accepted standards of technique, and yet have provided powerful and durable dramatic experiences. The problem is to find terms in which we can evaluate or describe an essentially subjective response.

One common basis for judgment is the "entertainment value" of a play, the degree to which it may or may not give pleasure. This criterion is one we instinctively employ, but it is not a satisfactory means of evaluating plays, both because our sources of pleasure are widely diverse and because the meaning of the term *pleasure* is extremely vague. How, for instance, are we to measure degrees of pleasure? We may laugh harder at a clown in the circus than at the witty and satirical barbs of a comedian, but does this mean we enjoy the experience more? We can watch a boxing match or a political convention on television, we can enjoy listening to a popular song or to a speech on international affairs, and we can see a track meet or participate in it; but how can we possibly compare the pleasures to be derived from such diverse activities? A frothy comedy by Noel Coward is a great deal more amusing than is *Hamlet,* but few people would seriously claim that in the long run it offers a more rewarding and satisfying experience.

What we need, obviously, is a more reliable measure of value than mere pleasure or entertainment. And the fact is that we do not ordinarily judge the value of our own experiences on the basis of whether or not they are "entertaining." Rather, we tend to see them as valuable or important in proportion to the intensity of the emotions they arouse and the degree to which we feel that they are organically and meaningfully related to the rest of our experience and to that of man as a whole. And if these are sound criteria for evaluating experience in general, they can be applied to drama also.

Drama, then, can be viewed as both the form and the response, as an entity wherein cause and effect are truly inseparable. In a tentative definition, we might say that a play is the re-creation or acting out of a unified series of events, a re-creation that, because of the order given those events and because of their apparent relevance to human life and problems, in turn creates both strong emotions and intellectual excitement.

The greatest danger in setting up any essentially subjective basis for judging drama is that we may seem to encourage critical relativism—the "every man his own critic" school of thought. The "my taste is as good as the next person's" attitude is quite natural and, up to a certain point, legitimate. Too often, however, it is the refuge of those who, out of laziness or lack of interest, would like to think that practice and experience have nothing to do with critical ability. If a reader or playgoer is left cold by a play that audiences and critics have found to be powerful and significant, he can assume that he has hopelessly bad taste or he can retreat behind the "I know what I like" defense. Or he can accept the fact that through inexperience with drama he has missed something that others have found, and know that with a little effort and practice he can find the same pleasure and satisfaction. Response to a play is individual, but not isolated and unique; it is proof of our common humanity.

Our use of subjective criteria for judging drama does not mean that we should, or even can, ignore the specifically structural elements, the component parts out of which the playwright constructs the experience we call a play. If a play is a failure, or if it has simply been less successful with its audience than some other play, it is often possible to trace the source of inferiority to weakness in structure, plotting, or characterization. This kind of post-mortem is worthwhile; it is both instructive and satisfying to try to analyze why a given play is better or worse than another. But dissection should come only after the fact. Obviously, it

would be a mistake to keep a critical eye on some isolated element in a play's structure while seeing or reading it and then
damn the whole because characterization, say, was faulty. The
test of any technique is whether it "works."

The analysis of structure is even more importantly used as an
aid to interpretation. Here again, analysis is a tool to be used only
after the initial and immediate impact of the dramatic experience,
after there has been a chance for a response relatively uncom-
plicated by self-conscious intellectualization. Many people
would like to think that they can leave drama at that, and leave
all further thinking about it to the professional critics; but the
person who is unwilling to think critically about drama will get
no more from his fiftieth play than he did from his first. Most
of us have felt, at one time or another, that a literary work—if
not a play, perhaps a poem or a story—contains something more
than immediately strikes the mind, some insight into the mystery
of human nature or the human situation that is powerful and
exciting but that we cannot quite grasp. It is just such a haunting
sense of depths unplumbed that has made *Hamlet* the most popular *and* the most analyzed literary work in English, and possibly in any language. Nearly any play that possesses the qualities
of intensity and relevance will inevitably have a third dimension,
mystery, which challenges the intellectually curious to search for
its hidden "heart."

And critical analysis, wisely used, is the most effective tool for
approaching the heart of a play. For while it is true that the precise nature of the dramatic experience is a personal matter, as
various as are the moods and background and tastes of the members of the audience, it is by no means completely free and individual. If the whole complex playwright-audience relationship is
successful, there are definite limits to the ways in which the individual may respond; and the limits are in large part defined by the
intentions of the playwright. On one level, obviously, he intends
to write a good play. Successful drama, however, is never merely
a series of such ordinary chaotic events as we witness daily in
our own lives. If the play has impact and vitality, it is because it

has been given direction and meaning by a coherent view of human experience. In other words, the form or structure of a play is the outgrowth and expression of the dramatist's vision or intentions, and, conversely, a study of the structure of a play will help the reader to a surer understanding of these intentions.

There is perhaps one difficulty in talking about the critical analysis of drama that needs to be cleared up. "Critical analysis" seems to suggest to some readers an elaborate machinery for the dissection and desiccation of plays, operated by those on the "inside" for the bafflement of outsiders. The notion that a play is some kind of puzzle or private code, and that the critic has in his possession a magic decoder pin that will solve the mystery, seems to lie behind the plaintive plea of many students: "But what am I supposed to be *looking* for in a play?"—as though there were a single vital clue that, once discovered, would illuminate the whole in a blinding flash. What the reader is "looking for," of course, is an experience, and the too-conscious search for some secret meaning can totally anesthetize the reader's sensitivity to the experience the playwright has to offer.

At the same time, that experience can be richer if the reader makes some effort to understand all the many things that may be going on in a play, all the things that the playwright is "doing." And in this respect there *is* a touchstone question, the answer to which will throw light on much in a play that might otherwise be misunderstood or ignored. It is, simply, the question "Why?"—asked again and again, every answer leading to a new question, until we have pushed back to the heart of the matter. This thread of "whys" can be picked up at almost any point in the fabric and followed until a pattern becomes clear. Nothing in a play is there by accident; everything is a part of the playwright's intention and can offer a clue to that design.

Why is some seemingly trivial incident included, or why this minor character? Why does a certain metaphor or symbol keep reappearing, or why does the play end on this particular note? And, in asking such questions, we should be investigating some particular technique not as an end in itself, but to see its place

What Is Drama?

in a larger pattern. The answers to our "whys" will usually lead to further questions. What, for instance, are the values that a character seems to embody or follow? How, if at all, are we to judge them? Does any conflict in values underlie the action of the play? Because a play has a plot and represents a connected and unified series of events, it contains a strong element of causality. In a sense, we are invited to observe the operation of cause and effect; and the relationship between what a character is—that is, the values by which he acts—and what he does or what happens to him is very often what the play is "about." In other words, the structure of a play, being the organization and interplay among its parts—the characters, their values, the conflict between these values and its outcome, the language, the setting, to name only a few—really constitutes its "meaning." And this structure will usually become clear if we ask "why" often enough.

But structure, however important, is still only a means to an end. It has already been suggested that drama is *both* the experience, of excitement or pleasure or new awareness, and the form —the arrangement of elements that gives substance and direction to that experience. The two components are inseparable, and in criticism an overemphasis upon either is apt to result in dehumanization on the one hand or careless and superficial impressionism on the other. But, since it is much easier, because more exact, to talk about form than about response, it is with form that a discussion of drama must begin, if not end.

ℋℋ Unique Qualities of Drama

There are many ways in which the reader can sharpen his awareness of the relationships between the form of the play and the probable intentions of the playwright. Perhaps the simplest as well as the most useful way is by making comparisons. By comparing plays with other forms of literature, and by comparing different kinds of drama with each other, we can learn a great deal

about why a dramatist chooses to express himself in a particular
form.

Of the two major literary genres, poetry and prose fiction, poetry bears the least apparent resemblance to drama. Yet, during most of its history since ancient Greece, drama has been considered simply one kind of poetry; until the nineteenth century many plays, and nearly all tragedies, were written in verse, and in their methods and their effects even many modern plays may legitimately be considered poetic. In other words, poetry is not only a genre, with various forms (lyric, epic, ballad, and so on), it is also a medium, a method of expression, that can be employed in other genres, such as drama. Since no meaningful contrast is possible, we might well leave the investigation of the dramatic uses of poetry until we consider some specific poetic plays.

Of the various forms of prose fiction, the novel, however, seems at first glance to be much like drama. Both a novel and a play, for instance, present some kind of story; and yet the *ways* in which the stories are presented are so disparate as to have almost no common ground. In the first place, the novel is a narrative—that is, it is told by someone rather than presented directly, as is a play. The novelist has, however, considerable flexibility in his choice of a narrator, depending upon his intentions and the kind of effect he wishes to create. The story may be told quite frankly by the novelist himself, or by one of the fictional characters in the novel. Or the narrator may be a disembodied, omniscient "spirit" who sees all but who is entirely outside the story and has no distinct personality. Choosing the omniscient point of view gives the author further flexibility in that it enables him to move at will in and out of the minds and most secret thoughts of as many characters as he may wish. This is an obvious advantage when the novelist wants to make clear the hidden and perhaps unconscious motives lying behind overt behavior that might otherwise be incomprehensible.

The novelist has also available, whatever his method of narration, the possibility of authorial comment, either on the significance of the action or on the nature of the people involved in it.

What Is Drama?

12   He can provide historical background, biographies of persons in the story, descriptions of places or events that lie outside the main action of the story—all of which can provide the reader with a richer, more complex experience.

In addition to freedom in the ways in which he can tell the story, the novelist has at his command almost unlimited control over space and time. He can, if he wishes, narrate events that are supposed to take place simultaneously, and he can shift his locale frequently and rapidly. He can move backward and forward in time at will and, what is perhaps much more important, he can set his own pace, dwelling for many pages on a single thought or reaction of a character, or hurrying in a few paragraphs over the events of days or even years.

These are only a few of the characteristic "advantages" that a novelist has over a dramatist. A dramatist cannot *tell* his story; he must show it—present it directly and physically on the stage. Although it is not quite accurate to say that a playwright must be more objective than a novelist, as far as presentation is concerned he must remain outside his story at all times. Unless he resorts to such essentially extra-dramatic devices as a prologue or choric commentary, he cannot normally intrude with his own opinions or with additional information, no matter how helpful it might be. In other words, drama has none of the characteristically discursive and descriptive qualities of the novel. The characters have to act out their own story, and all we can know of it is what they tell or show us. And they must do it within a temporal and spatial frame of reference that bears some relation to reality. There is no need to invoke the tired ghost of the "unities" of time and place, but it should be obvious that the dramatist's freedom to speed up or slow down chronology, to jump forward or backward in time, or to be in more than one place at once is seriously hampered by the physical presence of his characters.

On the other side of the ledger, however, drama has the advantages of immediacy, concentration, and intensity. The events happen, with all their disconcerting speed and harsh outlines, before our very eyes; and if we know less about the characters than we would in a novel, we need to know less, because they are living and acting in our very presence. A novel is usually a relatively leisurely affair; its effects are built up through many thousands of words and, for most people, through days of reading; and both involvement and conviction are gained through the depth of our intimacy with the characters. But a playwright has to respect the attention span of a theater audience and to get his job done in roughly two hours. These demands require, among other things, clarity—one might say simplicity, were it not too often confused with simple-mindedness. And clarity is usually achieved through tighter organization, more careful, or at least more obvious, attention to structure than is necessarily required of a novel. This emphasis on order and coherence is one of our sources of satisfaction in drama, both aesthetically, because of the pleasure we take in seeing a well-formed entity, and intellectually, because it suggests a pattern and meaning in human events that we do not ordinarily see in the workaday world. Thus it is that what drama seems to lose in detail and depth it gains in directness, in suggestiveness, and in focus.

This elemental and intense quality in drama goes back to its ritual beginnings in ancient Greece. The exact origin of drama is hidden in the past, and the earliest plays that have come down to us, those of Aeschylus, are already a sophisticated art form. There seems little doubt, however, that drama was associated with religious rites—with celebrating, or perhaps praying for, the end of winter and the return of the sun and spring. For these primitive and essentially agricultural people the cycles of the seasons and the cooperation of nature were the most important facts —and at the same time mysteries—of their existence. Whether these rituals were thought of as an acting out of their hopes or as attempts to appease powerful forces in an incomprehensible world, they represented a symbolic action on the part of the whole community, acknowledging the people's awe and terror in the face of what they could neither understand nor control, and at the same time their sense of identity with the elemental rhythms of nature.

What Is Drama?

Since the average modern playgoer is not vitally and personally concerned with the fertility of herds or the germination of crops, it would be difficult to claim that the ritualistic element in drama is quite the same today as it was in ancient Greece. Nevertheless, some of the characteristic features remain. In the theater, at least, drama is still a group experience, a community of people witnessing the acting out of their hopes and fears. And because we respond as a group and not simply as individuals, the laughter, the gasp, the half-repressed tear come more readily and, for some curious reason, the feelings are more intense. Perhaps this stronger response arises from the fact that we do feel ourselves part of the community, laughing or crying *for* that community. Or perhaps it occurs because for a moment we are released from the isolation of our individuality. Whatever the reason, the intensity and unanimity of the group's response suggests that, as in ritual, the play relates to the general, the typical, the symbolic aspects of man's experience, to whatever is of basic concern to the community, whether this is viewed as a society, as a civilization, or as all mankind.

Ritual consists, however, not simply of a response but also of the form that creates the response. Characteristically, the primitive ceremony represented the confrontation of mystery by the community, vicarious because "acted out" and yet imaginatively direct and concrete. Through ritual the individual, strengthened by his sense of identity with the group, could acknowledge the existence of what he could not explain or control; but ritual also provided a way in which he could come to terms with it. The heart of ritual, in its chants, in its dancing, even in its rudimentary drama, is its emphasis on rhythm and pattern, creating as it does at least the illusion that the mysteries it contemplates are part of an ordered and purposeful universe. And while later drama may be less concerned with man's gods, as representatives of natural or moral law, and more with making gods of the psychological and social forces that control men's destinies, the elements of form, rhythm, unity, still provides man with a barrier against chaos, a

The Nature and Kinds of "Reality" in Drama

refuge from the paralyzing possibility that what is beyond his understanding is meaningless.

Another reason for the intensity of both the ritual and the dramatic experience—and again something not available to narrative forms—is the physical presence of the actor. This is not simply a question of "realism," since no one really thinks that the actor is what he pretends to be; it is, rather, partly that the actor is a living person, and thus stresses the humanity of the event he enacts, and partly that the emotions of a human being, even when only "played," are highly contagious. Emotion begets emotion, and in the presence of strong feelings it is almost impossible to remain calm and detached, whether the reaction is sympathetic or the opposite. It is in part through his actors that a playwright controls the emotions, and consequently the experience, of his audience.

In addition to his actors, the dramatist has at his disposal the nonhuman but equally three-dimensional elements of the stage: all the rich possibilities of color and sound, of light and movement, of the entire physical theater. At the simplest level, lighting, setting, the volume and quality of the voices, possibly even music, can be used to establish the "tone" or mood of a scene. At a more sophisticated level, these elements, along with the physical placing of the actors with regard to each other or to the setting, and the use of gestures or movement, can be employed to suggest or symbolize unspoken and subtle relationships between individuals or groups.

Imagine, for instance, the staging of the second scene in Act I of a recent production of *Hamlet*. It is a key scene, for it is here, after the forebodings of the opening scene on the battlements, that we first meet most of the major figures in the play. The scene represents a state meeting of the court of Denmark, and as staged in this recent production, Claudius, Gertrude, and the courtiers enter with great pomp and circumstance amidst flourishes of trumpets, dipping flags, and frantic rearrangement of chairs and cushions by brightly clad flunkies. It is a vivid scene, full of color and bustle and noise. As the hubbub settles down, Claudius rises in his rich robes to address the court. We need hardly follow his words to hear in their complacent tones, or to see in his condescending gestures to his wife, to the courtiers, to Laertes, a man confident in his powers and secure in his position. The whole scene reflects this confidence: It fills the rear of the stage, brilliantly lit, colorful, loud, a little vulgar perhaps, as befits a man who need not care what people think, but withal dominated by a sense of pageantry and tradition and royalty.

But there is another figure in the scene, one we have all but overlooked. In his dark clothes, and placed well forward and to one side, he does not seem to be a part of the show and fine words; it is as though he had wandered into the world of Claudius and his court quite by accident. Nor does he give it any attention, as though it did not exist for him, until Claudius nods graciously in his direction: "But now, my cousin Hamlet, and my son." With Hamlet's reply, the focus of the scene shifts to him; but before he has said a word we sense his isolation, his melancholy, his profound distrust of Claudius and the whole world of the court. In other words, a state of mind that is manifest throughout the first half of the play, and that is stated explicitly in Hamlet's soliloquies, is made visually and powerfully evident the first time we see him.

With Hamlet's muttered reply to Claudius: "A little more than kin, and less than kind," the whole mood of the scene begins to change, as though the bitterness implicit in it has tainted the gay, garish, secure world of the court. Its brightness is dimmed, the flags droop, the trumpets are silent—until Claudius, in a desperate effort to reassert his dominance, leaves in a burst of noise— movement and bustle stop, the courtiers mutter uneasily among themselves, and the tone of the speeches becomes querulous. The brilliance and power suggested by the first part of the scene have faded, as the condescending self-confidence of the King has been shaken, and Hamlet gradually takes over the scene until, after the court has departed far less impressively than it arrived, he and his dark brooding are left alone on the stage. In this one scene, then,

The Nature and Kinds of "Reality" in Drama

much that is basic to the play, in terms of our understanding of character, relationships, states of mind, as well as forebodings of the future, is suggested symbolically by nonverbal elements in the production.

But while the purely theatrical elements, the living actors and the physical stage, can be used in many ways to underline and clarify what is going on in a play and to intensify the effectiveness of the experience as a whole, they cannot exist by themselves; the essential element in drama is still words. The importance of language will be apparent if we compare drama with its "sister" dramatic art, motion pictures. Indeed, one might well wonder whether the movies are a literary, or verbal, art at all. Anyone who has watched one of the old silent films or has watched a movie on television without benefit of sound will realize that, while words may be useful, they often are not essential. In the case of most plays that are translated into movies, we find that much of the dialogue is either radically altered or simply left out, and a great amount of what had been *said* is now *shown*. It is perfectly reasonable that this difference should exist, since the peculiar virtues of the film medium are flexibility, intimacy, and range. It can let us see so much more than any stage: It can show a vast panorama of snow-capped mountains or the tiniest wild-flower on one of the peaks; it can show the whole grim spectacle of a great battle, or it can focus on the frightened eyes of a man who sees death; it can move from the superhuman to the sub-human at the blink of an eye; and it can, for purposes of humor or suspense or powerful irony, juxtapose the most incongruous and widely separated scenes. In the realm of the visual, its powers are almost unlimited, and it is generally when it exploits that realm to the utmost that the film comes closest to being an art.

A comparison between the text of a play and the shooting script of a movie (which consists largely of directions for the camera and sound-effect crews) will reveal the extent to which the film director relies on visual and aural elements to create his effects, whereas the playwright depends on the power and sug-gestiveness of words. It is for this reason, of course, that a play

18   can be read with relatively little loss in effect, while a movie
cannot. But it might well be imagined that the movies, because of
the variety of their appeal to the senses—especially the visual—
should be the richest and most flexible of all art forms; and indeed
they have a tremendous but largely unrealized potential. The
principal virtue of the form, however, is also its greatest limitation. If the old cliché that a picture is worth a thousand words
were unqualifiedly true, then doubtless the movies would be the
highest form of art. But it is true only in the sense that a picture
can show or present the scene itself, in all its concrete details,
better than mere verbal description can do. The artist, however,
would often rather *suggest* than show, and words can be infinitely
more suggestive than pictures. The haunting regret of Villon's
"Ou sont les neiges d'antan," or the emptiness and despair of
Macbeth's "Tomorrow and tomorrow and tomorrow. . ." could
not be replaced by a thousand pictures. For pictures are too particular, too limited by what is there, while the suggestiveness of
language can stimulate the imagination to go far beyond anything
the combined efforts of director, cameraman, and special-effects
department could produce. Words are still man's richest and most
subtle means of communication; and, since drama is a verbal
art, with visual reinforcement, it will probably always be able to
do some things movies cannot, just as movies do things plays
cannot.

The really distinctive feature of motion pictures, however, is
not that they appeal to several senses at once—a play seen in the
theater does that—but that they can take us out of ourselves in a
way that a play cannot. Sitting in a totally dark movie theater, we
are hypnotized by the brilliant screen before us. The movie
reaches out and detaches us from the everyday world and makes
us a part of its own unreal reality. Because of its great visual
impact, the experience of the films can often be as intense and
convincing as that of drama; and because of its hypnotic quality
it has no need, in order to engage our attention, to rely upon our
sense of relevance to common human problems, or upon issues
important to us. As a result, the movies are the natural medium

for the entertainment of escape, pure and simple, and the movie-makers have never been reluctant to capitalize on this fact. But while all art is in some sense escapist, one basis for judging it is the extent to which the world we escape *into* enriches or illuminates the world we escape *from*.

Since television provides most Americans with their most frequent contact with dramatic entertainment, something should be said of that medium. In general, both plays and movies offer a less satisfactory experience on television than they do in the theaters for which they were designed. Stage drama seems strangely cold and stilted on the screen where we have just viewed newsreel shots of a riot or of an airplane wreck, while movies lose both the impressive scope of their giant-sized screen and the hypnotic element of their theater in the tiny world of the television set. The best television drama is usually that written expressly for the medium, written with an eye to its unique limitations and possibilities.

The real virtues of television, however, lie not in drama but in the world of first-hand experience—in spotting a prime minister as he climbs off a plane, in permitting us to witness a political convention or a natural disaster, in making us spectators at a sporting event. Here is drama of a different sort—a kind that no other medium can capture so well.

Since we have already moved a long way from dramatic literature, and since we have spoken of athletic events as "drama," it may not be so foolish as it perhaps seems, to consider what common ground there may be that permits us to speak of both plays and such things as a particularly tense baseball game or an upset finish in football as "dramatic." The most obvious element that they share is conflict, the basic element of all drama. But the existence of conflict is not enough in itself to justify the analogy. It is entirely possible for us to find a sports event thoroughly satisfactory in which our whole attention is devoted to observing the skill of the participants, regardless of who wins, while it would be hard to imagine a play in which we were aware only of the skill of the actors. A play is not merely a display of technical profi-

What Is Drama?

ciency; and, by the same token, an event is not dramatic if the pleasure is primarily that of observing a skillful performance. In order for drama to exist, we must have not only conflict but also a feeling that in the conflict something is at stake; we must take sides and become involved.

Why is it that almost every day between April and October hundreds of thousands of reasonably intelligent Americans crowd into stadiums all over the country and work themselves into a state of wild excitement over a game of baseball? Not chiefly because we get a thrill from a game well played, not even because we may have money wagered on the result, but because we care who wins. Whether the fact that we care is a form of escapism is unimportant; for the time being at least, one team is *our* team, representing our city, our college, our section of the country. Success justifies us, our pride in the community, and our faith in the team, and defeat—so intensely do we care at the time— seems a clear instance of the triumph of injustice and evil.

It is in much the same sense that we "identify" with characters in a play. The concept of identification is sometimes misunderstood to mean that we somehow imagine ourselves in the shoes of the most sympathetic figure; but this is patent nonsense. Our interest in a baseball game does not depend on the illusion that we are on the field ourselves, nor does our involvement in a play arise from our imagining that we are taking part in the action. "Identifying" means simply that in a play there is usually one character (the protagonist)—though there may be more than one —who we feel represents us, who in at least some respects stands for what we stand for, our hopes, our beliefs, our point of view. The conflict of the play is thus in some way a challenge to us and to what we hope is "true"; the success of our protagonist, like the victory of our team, is a reinforcement and justification of our beliefs; his failure throws them in doubt. In either case, it is because his values are ours, and both are in danger, that we become involved in drama.

But, while a spectator sport may be in this crude sense dramatic and may represent a relatively intense experience, it certainly is

The Nature and Kinds of "Reality" in Drama

not drama. And the reasons for this are not so obvious as they seem. Of course, there is little language—at least that is printable —but, more important, there is no script and no plot. A game, in other words, is essentially unstructured. Neither we nor the players know how it will come out; if we did, no one would watch it. It has no fixed and permanent form, created by a single conscious mind; once it happens it will never be again, and what happens during the course of it is largely a matter of chance. A play, on the other hand, does have a design, given it by a creator. It involves a conscious structuring of events based on a particular view of life; it is an ordering of experience for the purpose of making some comment *on* experience. But a game, because it is undirected, cannot be a comment on anything, except perhaps the ability of the players. In spite of our identification with a particular team, its victory or defeat has nothing whatever to do with the values or beliefs or ideals of Duke University or Kansas City or the Trinity Church bowling team. If our team wins, it does so through skill and chance, not virtue. A game, then, has reference to nothing significant outside itself.

A statement such as the last raises the age-old problem of the relationship of entertainment to art and will always provoke someone to assert belligerently, "I go to a play to be amused, not to learn something." This is a perfectly legitimate attitude; but it is usually based on a profound misunderstanding of the sense in which art is significant and meaningful. If drama teaches anything or has any meaning, it is only in the same sense that an experience in real life can be instructive and meaningful, except that we can always leave the theater when the play is over. But to a great degree it is just this process of "learning" that gives the pleasure in drama. Only when the problems faced by the characters, and the values or issues at stake in the central conflict, seem real and important can we become sufficiently involved in the play for it to *be* an experience. And it is, to a great extent, the involvement of an experience that will make a play truly satisfying, and therefore pleasurable. The relevance of a play to basic human concerns is a source of its pleasure; and, by the same token, without the pleasure there would be no real meaning.

Perhaps this is equivalent to saying that, as long as a play deals with beings or situations that are recognizably human, it is virtually impossible for it not to have meaning. It is possible, nevertheless, to speak in terms of degrees of meaningfulness. It is perfectly true, of course, that a clever playwright might have the audience of a trivial play bathed in tears or weak from laughter; but the final criterion of effectiveness (and therefore "meaning") is not the violence of the emotion but its durability. The play that stays with us beyond the limits of the theater, the play to which we can return again and again with no sense of diminished power and depth, is far more satisfying as total dramatic experience than a good cry or a good laugh, left behind in the darkness of the theater. And the play that seems richer, more perceptive of the human condition each time we see or read it, is the truly great play.

𝕏𝕏𝕏 Types of Drama

Looking at the dramatic experience in terms of its reference to the aspects of life outside itself offers a basis for our last set of comparisons: the differences among the various types or categories into which plays are usually divided. These labels are rather clumsy generalizations, but they do provide us a useful vocabulary for talking about distinctions between plays. The common classifications are melodrama, farce, comedy, tragicomedy, and tragedy. It is possible to make infinite refinements upon this list, so that it includes satire, the "problem" play, sentimental comedy, or even Polonius' "tragical-comical-historical-pastoral"; but for our purposes the five mentioned categories will suffice.

The categories are least satisfactory when applied to contemporary drama, and in some cases they break down altogether. Motivated partly by the desire to experiment and, hence, to break away from traditional modes, partly by an awareness that life itself does not fit neatly into "comic" or "tragic" patterns, and partly by new concepts of what drama "is," some dramatists in the twentieth century have consciously written plays that cannot possibly be defined by conventional terminology. The so-called Theater of the Absurd, notably in the works of Beckett and Ionesco, includes several plays that are at once farcical and bitter and serious, if not tragic. However, since many playwrights today and most in the past thought and wrote in terms of reasonably well-defined "types" of plays, the five classifications still provide a useful and valid way of talking about most drama.

While these types do not always exist in a pure form, the characteristics of each are readily identifiable, and one usually provides the dominant tone or attitude of any given play. Probably the easiest to spot are those—melodrama and farce—that would normally stand at the bottom of any scale of "meaningfulness." This does not mean that it is wrong or shows bad taste to enjoy melodrama and farce; these forms of drama can often provide an evening's entertainment for the most sophisticated and intellectual palate. As dramatic experiences, however, plays of these types are least important, least durable, have the least relevance to anything outside themselves. Indeed, this lack of reference to anything significant outside its own limited and artificial world might be taken as a definition of either melodrama or farce; they are in a sense theatrical equivalents of the baseball game.

The elements characteristic of melodrama are excitement and suspense, as the hero skillfully evades destruction at every turn and ultimately emerges triumphant over the forces of evil— largely through sheer good luck. The appeal springs from action and adventure, with plenty of thrills and chills, a touch of romance, and a happy ending. We become involved because we identify ourselves with the protagonist, who is likely to be a somewhat idealized version of our day-dream image of ourselves; but what happens to him usually has very little to do with what he *is*, with his personality or his view of life. Again, there is nothing wrong with action and suspense—almost any play needs them to keep our attention; but melodrama has little more than these. For this reason, melodrama does not wear well; once seen, its effect and its "meaning" have been exhausted.

Many serious plays, however, possess all the external features of melodrama without falling into that category. *Romeo and Juliet,* for instance, has riots, murder, duels, midnight assignations, a missent letter, and a double suicide. Nothing could be more melodramatic, and yet the focus of the play is not simply on the excitement and suspense. Indeed, Shakespeare undercuts the element of suspense by telling the tragic outcome of the story in the "Chorus" that opens the play, as though to turn our attention from merely *what* happens to *why* it happens.

Farce bears much the same relation to comedy that melodrama has to serious drama or to tragedy. Just as the interest in melodrama arises from action and suspense, so the comic element in farce derives largely from "funny" and incongruous situations. Farce usually depends heavily on puns, "sight gags," and surprise for its effect; on plot and incident rather than character, on "what" rather than "why." And, like melodrama, farce rarely has much to do with the world outside the theater.

It is not necessary to go into all the scholarly attempts to define the nature of comedy or the comic spirit in order to recognize comedy when we see it on the stage. Farce is, of course, comic; but, whereas farce has little relevance to the real world, comedy, as the term is used here, does have. Comedy might be described as the humorous or light or nonserious treatment of a potentially serious subject. This does not really define comedy, because it does not indicate the sources of the humor; but these are as varied as the ingenuity of man. Sometimes, indeed, the humor will lie simply in the incongruity of handling serious matters in a light-hearted or irreverent way. The important point, however, is that the tone or attitude of the treatment, rather than the subject matter itself, is the characteristic quality that distinguishes comedy from noncomic drama. For instance, the ease with which a man can be made jealous of his wife is treated seriously in *Othello*

(1604)[1] but is one of the many subjects treated comically in Ben Jonson's *Volpone* (1606). There is, in fact, almost no subject too serious to be handled comically—death, adultery, religion, crime, poverty, the vanity of human dreams.

The paradox that lies at the heart of comedy is that it is serious and not serious at the same time. The situations must seem threatening enough to engage our interest, but at the same time we must be able to view them as capable of resolution without harmful consequences. The issues at stake in the conflict must be enough our own that we identify our hopes and fears, if not with those of a particular protagonist, at least with the implied point of view of the playwright; yet the conflict must not involve our emotions to the degree that we lose the power of objective and rational judgment. Sometimes, this balance between detachment and emotional response may be upset, usually at the expense of the comic element. In *Volpone,* for instance, some of the characters are so incredibly selfish, so thoroughly despicable, that they cease to be comic figures; or, in the same play, the punishment meted out to the engaging rascal Mosca may seem so severe that the fun of the ending is somewhat spoiled. While these are relatively minor blemishes in an excellent play, they point up the fact that the successful writer of comedy must tread a fine line between evoking too little or too great involvement on the part of his audience.

The various devices that a playwright uses to insure this detachment are among the most characteristic techniques of comedy. As we have already seen, we become involved in a play partly to the degree to which we are convinced that the characters and their problems are "real"; comedy, consequently, is in the ambiguous position of striving to be at once real and unreal. Since farce is by definition divorced from reality, many of the elements used in comedy to maintain the sense of distance are farcical in nature. In *Twelfth Night* (*ca.* 1600), for example, it is only because he is the victim of farcical and implausible pranks that

---

[1] Dates given in the text are those of first performance or, where that is unknown, of publication.

Malvolio is kept from being a genuinely pathetic figure; at the same time, the farce does not take over, and Malvolio remains the embodiment of self-delusion, a very real and human failing, one of the central concerns of the play as a whole.

Exaggeration, a characteristic device of farce, is another technique often used to keep us from getting too close to the characters or situations of comedy. The extravagant obesity of Falstaff in *Henry IV* (*ca.* 1597) is the source of endless jokes and farcical situations, but it also prevents us from taking too seriously qualities in the man that, from another point of view, might be seen as vicious. Witty dialogue and repartee, such as were never spoken by humans in the real world, can be both a source of humor in themselves and a means of keeping the audience detached. Dorimant, in Sir George Etherege's *Man of Mode* (1676), along with most of the "heroes" of Restoration comedy, would seem nothing but a vicious and dissolute debauchee were not our moral judgment, which would damn him in the real world, at least partially dulled by his brilliant wit. Finally, a more general method of keeping us from becoming too deeply involved is the playwright's encouragement of a sense of superiority to the characters on the part of the audience. As far back as Aristotle, it was recognized that comedy should deal with people who are "less" than average. It does not matter in exactly what sense they are inferior to us; but being able to look down on them provides us a sense of satisfaction at the same time that it keeps us from taking them too seriously.

The comic view of life is essentially rational, in the sense that it generally sees reason as man's most valuable attribute. We have already seen that comedy is made up of paradoxes; one of them is that its view is both pessimistic and optimistic. It emphasizes man's frailty, seeing him as weak, deluded, even vicious; at the same time, it usually manifests a faith that with common sense, good humor, and a mature and realistic view of ourselves and of life these defects can be either overcome or rendered harmless. Because of this assumption that man may remedy many of his imperfections through the exercise of his rational nature, much of comedy is, in theory at least, corrective. Satire, which is perhaps the commonest form that comedy takes, undertakes to ridicule the follies of mankind, to laugh man's selfishness and self-delusion and pride out of fashion.

Not all comedy, however, is as didactic as satire tends to be. Romantic comedy (such as *Twelfth Night*) and the comedy of manners (such as Congreve's *Way of the World*, 1700) are not usually concerned with changing human nature but are willing to take our frailty as a given condition of existence and to have some fun with it. But even here the source of fun is, in a broad sense, the characters' confusion of appearance and reality, their inability to see things as they are. If he could see clearly, rather than through the distorting lenses of his romantic dreams or his sense of his own importance, if he had a rational and whole view of the world, man might not be perfect, but he would be better able to adjust the reality of his nature to the reality of the world he is in. And, of course, there would be no comedy. The comic view of life sees man as limited but regards his limitations as serious only so long as he cannot see and accept them. The paradoxical nature of man can, in this view, be resolved through humor and good sense.

Tragedy, too, is concerned with paradoxes and limitations, but in tragedy the paradoxes cannot be resolved and the limitations will not be accepted. *Tragedy* is probably the most often and ill defined term in dramatic literature. Writers on the subject tend either to be guilty of special pleading, defining the term so narrowly that it will fit only their favorite tragedies, or to describe it so broadly as to be of no help at all. Chaucer's Monk, in *The Canterbury Tales*, says that tragedies are tales of men "y-fallen out of heigh degree into miserie." This is doubtless true as far as it goes, but it does not say anything about what kind of men or why they "fall," and one can think of many examples fulfilling the terms of the definition, such as the defeat of Hitler, that would scarcely be called tragic. At the other extreme, the hypothetical man in the street would probably say that a tragedy is a story with a sad ending. This definition obviously suffers from the same vagueness—a happy marriage that ended in the divorce courts might well be sad

What Is Drama?

without being tragic. Both these efforts, however crude, suggest one of the problems facing any attempt at definition: Does *tragedy* refer to a particular kind of subject matter or to a specific emotional response on the part of the audience?

Aristotle, whose definition of tragedy has survived time and changes in taste remarkably well, said *both*: that ideally tragedy should have as its hero a man of some eminence, better than average morally but possessing some "flaw," who suffers a reversal in fortune ending in misery or death, and that his story should arouse and effect the purgation of the emotions of pity and fear. Sound as this definition has proved to be, it is still too general to be of much help in giving us a basis for evaluating tragedy; for deciding what makes one play sucessful and another not, or for deciding why the catharsis of pity and fear should be pleasurable.

One way to get at an understanding of tragedy is to compare it with comedy and with the "in-between" form, tragicomedy. The label *tragicomedy* is derived from the most elementary definition of the component terms: that tragedy is concerned with unhappy or pathetic events, and that comedy ends happily; but in fact tragicomedy is neither tragic nor comic. Conventionally, a play of this type will set up a serious and potentially tragic or at least dangerous situation, develop it for four acts, and then, usually by a bit of sleight of hand, provide a happy ending. Actually, a tragicomedy is very like melodrama, except that the problems it deals with are—or at least seem—real and meaningful; but, as in melodrama, they are resolved unexpectedly by chance or by the fortunate intrusion at the last minute of some person heretofore outside the story.

Tragicomedy might be described as a kind of "emotional gymnasium." In it our emotions are aroused—often powerfully—and then released through a fortuitous resolution that evades the issues raised, in the sense that it provides an answer too easy to be genuinely convincing. It is as though the playwright were incapable of sustaining the tensions he has raised to a truly tragic outcome, or of facing the logical conclusion of his own premises. This type of drama seems to operate, where the emotions are

The Nature and Kinds of "Reality" in Drama

concerned, on a kind of "have your cake and eat it too" principle:
We have the pleasure of suspense, premonitions of disaster, and a kind of pseudo-fear that are carefully laid to rest in the ending, and we are sent out feeling, presumably, that everything can work out for the best after all.

It should not be assumed, however, that the *deus ex machina*[2] is used only by a careless or incompetent playwright. In a small number of plays, mostly comedies, the use of this device actually intensifies the effect of the ending. In Molière's *Tartuffe* (1664), for example, after the hypocritical Tartuffe has wormed his way into possession of Monsieur Orgon's home and fortune and has thrown his erstwhile benefactor into the streets, King Louis (who, it turns out, has had his eye on Tartuffe all along) intervenes, has the rascal thrown into jail, and returns his loot to a sadder and wiser Orgon. The play is a satiric comedy and of course has to end happily; but this solution is so frankly implausible that we are forced to recognize the tragic consequences of Orgon's blindness had the King not intervened. The obvious falsity of the ending, in other words, provides the comedy with tragic undertones; we cannot avoid the awareness that in the real world the situation could not have been resolved so neatly.

And the essence of the tragic view is the awareness that things do *not* work out for the best, that present in the nature of things are inherent limitations, which, in spite of our best efforts, render our fondest hopes and dreams futile delusions; and yet man continues to hope and dream.

If comedy takes an essentially rational view of man and assumes that the undeluded mind is adequate to resolve most of his problems, tragedy is nonrational, both in the sense that its effect depends on a high degree of emotional involvement and, more important, in that it acknowledges that reason and virtue are *not* enough, that the human situation represents a paradox and a dilemma with which the intellect cannot cope. If comedy assumes

[2] Literally, "the god out of the machine"—referring to a device, sometimes used by the ancient Greeks, by which one of the Olympian gods was lowered onto the stage to provide a satisfactory resolution to a play. Today, the phrase is often used to describe a contrived and unconvincing ending.

What Is Drama?

that man can come to terms with life and its limitations, tragedy recognizes that he often cannot. And if the effect of comedy depends on its ability to clarify the truth, to reveal man to himself, the effect of tragedy springs from its acceptance of the very incomprehensibility and mystery of life.

Tragedy may have many forms and subjects, but nearly all that have proved successful, that have been able to move men in certain ways, have conspicuous elements in common. At the most basic level, the mysteries contemplated in tragedy are the insoluble paradoxes and contradictions of human experience: the mystery of a life that seems to hold out unlimited possibilities of happiness and power but that is hedged round by death and darkness; the mystery of men who "pray as though they would die tomorrow, and work as though they would live forever." Tragedy is the mystery of men who know intellectually the limitations of reason and mortality but refuse to accept them; of men who know that they must bear the consequences of what they do, yet can do nothing else and still be men. Or it is the mystery of men who would do well, and who are faced with mutually exclusive obligations; who have had laid on them absolute demands of duty, loyalty, love, and morality that are absolutely irreconcilable.

This is a very general way of talking about tragedy, but it must be, because man's notions about the nature of his limitations or about the values he is expected to live up to change from age to age. The central contradictions of life, however, remain unchanged. In Greek tragedy, for instance, the inherent limitations and conflicting obligations of man's existence are represented by the Olympian gods. In Sophocles' *Oedipus* the doom pronounced by the gods cannot be escaped by any effort of will or reason; and in Euripides' *Hippolytus* Aphrodite and Artemis suggest the irreconcilable demands of love and chastity. In medieval tragedy the wills of the gods were replaced by the Wheel of Fortune, which symbolized the instability of all earthly happiness and good fortune and was regarded as God's reproof of worldly ambition and vanity. In such an expressly Christian frame of reference, where man's limitations and disappointments are not only accepted but welcomed as part of God's goodness, tragedy is virtually impossible, and the Middle Ages produced almost none.

The Renaissance, with its reawakened interest in man as a mortal rather than an immortal being, paid particular attention in its tragedy to limitations inherent in man's own nature. Shakespeare, for instance, was fascinated by the idea that the very qualities responsible for man's power and nobility and goodness are also the source of his weakness and failure. We can see this first in *Romeo and Juliet* (*ca.* 1595), where the mystery is a double paradox: that the same youthful impetuosity which makes possible that passionate and precipitous love between the two is also the source of their destruction, and in part that the most perfect expression of love is the renunciation of that life without which love cannot exist. In *King Lear* (1606) the qualities that have made Lear a strong king make him a weak father; and it is Cordelia's great love that is the source of her fatal silence. It is Othello's very virtue and innocence that Iago turns to blackest pitch. And it is not mere feeble vacillation and "inability to make up his mind" that keeps Hamlet from acting until the power of choice is taken out of his hands, but a conscientious desire to do what is right in a world where a clear and simple "right" is not to be found.

The modern period, continuing the humanistic tradition of the Renaissance, has become particularly interested in man as a social being, and so its tragedy, from Ibsen to Arthur Miller, has dealt largely with the inescapable but irreconcilable conflict between the demands of society, in the form of family, church, community, or nation, and the need of the individual to "be himself." Ibsen's *Ghosts* (1881) concerns a woman who, in conforming to her community's concept of morality, denies a more basic and more "real" morality, with terrifying consequences. Arthur Miller's Willy Loman, in *Death of a Salesman* (1949), accepts without question the mores and values of the contemporary urban commercial world, although he has a haunting sense that something is wrong. And the very qualities that would have made him happy and successful as a farmer or a carpenter destroy him as a

What Is Drama?

salesman. "He had the wrong dreams," his son says at the end; but Willy had answered him earlier: In twentieth-century America, what other dreams can a man have?[3]

It is sometimes said that in comedy man lacks freedom of choice, and that tragedy depends upon his having free will. If this is true, it is only in the sense that within the context of comedy man has surrendered his freedom to his folly and self-delusion, and that the effect of tragedy depends on our feeling that he is something more than a shuttlecock of fate. But the implications of comedy are that man *can* direct his life through the exercise of reason; in tragedy his choice is, in a sense, only an illusion. Man defies this lack of freedom—and that is his glory; but, ultimately, his choice is only whether he will take defeat lying down or fighting.

Tragedy, like comedy, is made up of contradictions, and perhaps the greatest of these is that we should find pleasurable the prospect of man's inevitable defeat in the face of insurmountable dilemmas and frustrations. And it is a demonstrable fact of dramatic history that through the ages successful tragedy has been both the most difficult kind of drama to write and the most satisfying to experience. But, although the empirical evidence is there, in our own experience and in that of millions of others, it is not at all clear exactly what makes tragedy satisfying.

Sometimes it is said that one of the pleasures of tragedy is the satisfaction we feel that the calamity we are witnessing is not happening to us. This is not only a rather petty response, one not worthy of tragedy, but it is simply not true. If tragedy offers relief at all, it is only as an escape from the element of forced gaiety and false optimism in our culture, which says "all's right with the world" when in fact we know it is not. A feeling of gratification that we are not the persons participating in the events of the play may arise in comedy; the intensity of tragedy, however, springs in large part from our awareness that we *are* the people in the play. In melodrama, much of our excitement comes from the

[3] In *Four Modern Plays* (New York: Rinehart & Company, Inc., 1958), p. 337.

The Nature and Kinds of "Reality" in Drama

hair-raising events that are happening before us, implausible as they may be to our cooler judgment. But in tragedy our emotions do not really arise from the fact that what we are seeing *is* happening so much as from the realization that it *could* happen. Our sorrow is not for the people on the stage, but for ourselves.[4]

There is always pleasure in what is true and authentic, in the feeling that the playwright has broken through the unstructured chaos of everyday experience and has shown us some elemental pattern we sensed but never quite saw, grim and painful though it may be. He thus gives form and coherence to what is incomprehensible. And the satisfaction we may find in tragedy does not come from any answers he offers to our questions. The tragic dramatist does not tell us why death exists to rob our ambitions of meaning; why limitations exist that keep men not from wanting, but only from getting; why we are torn between conflicting obligations. All he does is make us feel the existence and the pathos of these mysteries. At the same time, he reassures us that, in our sense of bafflement and helplessness before them, we are not alone. Others, indeed all mankind, have faced the same enigmas. Indeed, much of the sorrow of tragedy is offset by a complementary sense of awe at the defiance and dignity that man *can* show before overwhelming odds, when he acts as though his powers were unlimited, not through ignorance but through courage.

There is some sadness in tragedy, at the helplessness and hopelessness of man's fate; there is much awe, at the prospect of the clash of mighty opposites—the individual, in all his dignity and defiance, against all the enigmatic and implacable forces, both within and without, that baffle and thwart him; and there is even joy, that we too are members of the human race and part of the drama.

[4] This is perhaps what Aristotle meant by "pity and fear."

What Is Drama?

THE MEANING OF "REALITY" IN DRAMA

⚏ The Multiplicity of "Reality"

In the last chapter the terms *real* and *reality* were used freely and with assurance, as though it were perfectly obvious what they meant. And for everyday uses the meaning probably is sufficiently clear; we would say that reality is "something that really *is*," or, to use the dictionary phrase, something "having actuality," and be happy to leave more abstruse speculations to the professional philosophers. The hopeless circularity of these supposed "definitions" need bother us only if we are forced to clarify our thinking further. Since it has been asserted that the effectiveness and the "meaning" of drama depend on its contact with "reality," we do need to come to a more precise agreement as to the meaning of the word. Indeed, lack of such agreement is probably the greatest single barrier to communication between a playwright and his audience.

The exact distinction between what is real and what is not is far from clear, however. It is obviously not sufficient to say that only that is real which is subject to perception and measurement. The *effects* of love and hate can perhaps be perceived, but the emotions themselves can be neither seen nor submitted to a scale. Nor can we even say that in order to be real an entity must

36   exist; for in what sense do abstractions, such as justice or honor or truth, or even reality itself, have existence? Is "evil" simply an abstraction; or is it a "thing" that has existence; or is it neither, but simply the absence of good? And, for that matter, in what sense is "good" real?

On a more physical level: Can a sound be said to exist if no one hears it? We sometimes hear people credited with being really good-natured behind a harsh manner, or with being clever and never showing it; but can we say that these qualities are real if no one can perceive them? And what of the medically proven cases of people who, without any observable physiological basis, have been so convinced of their own sickness that they reveal all the overt symptoms of a disease? Is their illness real or not?

When we have fallen out of love with someone, it is perfectly natural for us to feel, with complete conviction, that we were never truly in love at all. Can a mere change of feeling make that unreal which was real before? When two individuals perceive the same event entirely differently, as often happens, are *both* perceptions real? Is a dream real, or is it a hallucination? If it is unreal, why? And what is the real "us"? Is it the image we have of ourselves, colored and distorted as it must be by our vision of what we would *like* to be, or is it a composite of all that others see in us? To put it more simply, is "reality" objective or subjective?

This barrage of questions and speculations, which could go on indefinitely, is not intended simply to confuse the reader, nor need the questions be answered before we can go further; we can proceed without knowing exactly what reality is. It is necessary, at this point, only to be aware that what is real may be conceived of in several possible ways. This awareness is essential to any investigation of the meaning and function of reality in drama.

Appearance as Reality

One of the terms heard most frequently in discussions of modern drama is *realism*. This term refers to the theory that art in general, or drama in particular, should conform to reality. If taken literally, the term should be as varied in its implications as is the parent word. In actual practice, however, the concept of realism has acquired a somewhat more specific meaning, referring to that principle of playwriting, acting, and production which holds as its ideal the most literal possible translation of life onto the stage. In its extreme form this is sometimes known as "slice-of-life" realism, a term suggesting the random selection of a cross section of life in the raw, as it were, in all its formlessness and chaos. But even when the playwright exercises considerable powers of selectivity, the objective of realism remains the most accurate possible reproduction of the familiar world visually, psychologically, in language and motivation—indeed, by every means that will strengthen the illusion of literal, observable reality.

An impulse toward realism can be found in some degree in the drama of almost every period. A development in this direction can be seen in classical Greek drama, in the works, successively, of Aeschylus, Sophocles, and Euripides. In the degenerate Roman dramatic form of the mime it was often carried to crude and even brutal extremes, as when a condemned criminal would occasionally be forced to play a role in order that an execution or murder might be literally authentic. Part of the impetus behind medieval religious drama—to which modern drama owes an immense debt—was the desire to make the stories of Christ's life more real and therefore more comprehensible to an illiterate audience. Many of the figures in the early "craft cycles," such as the shepherds in *The Second Shepherds' Play,* step not out of the pages of the Bible but out of contemporary fifteenth-century England.

It was in part the popular appeal of realistic accuracy that led many London theaters of the early nineteenth century to produce elaborate historical spectacles, such as *The Siege of Gibraltar,* which was billed as "an exact representation of the armament by Land and Sea, of the combined forces of France and Spain, with real Men of War and Floating Batteries, built and rigged by pro-

The Meaning of "Reality" in Drama

fessional men from his Majesty's Dock Yards, and which float in a receptacle containing nearly 8000 cubic feet of real water."[1]

In the history of drama the term *realism* has, however, come to be associated specifically with the revulsion, beginning in the late nineteenth century, against the blatant falsity and artificiality of the shoddy romantic comedies, melodramas, and so-called well-made plays that had dominated the stage for half a century or more. These plays were "unreal" in any of a number of ways. The characters were too often mere two-dimensional stereotypes, dramatic clichés of the most monotonous kind. The plots were frequently ingenious and involved—to such a degree that the machinery needed to unravel them sometimes creaked audibly; and one suspects that the principal pleasure to be derived from such plays lay in watching the cleverness of the playwright as he entangled himself in impossible situations and then extricated himself, rather than in seeing any just or valid representation of humanity. Both language and acting techniques were so stiff and stylized that the plays would be laughed off the stage today. Some idea of the dramatic fare of the day is suggested by a sampling of titles appearing in London theaters at mid-century: *Belinda the Blind, or The Stepmother's Vengeance; The Idiot Queen, or The Chapel of Miracles* (one title was never considered sufficient); *Jane Paul, or The Victim of Unmerited Persecution; The Spectre Bridegroom, or A Ghost in Spite of Himself.*

The stage, in other words, was peopled with unbelievable characters speaking an inhuman tongue in an unconvincing setting. The reaction against this state of affairs began quietly enough, in various improvements in the purely visual aspects of stage production. The introduction of gas and later of electricity permitted a vastly increased range and flexibility in lighting ef-

---

[1] The accuracy of this advertisement may well be questioned, since the "receptacle" in question measured forty by one hundred feet and was two feet deep—not enough for even a single very small man-of-war. This anonymous spectacle appeared at the Sadler's Wells Theatre in 1804. The handbill is quoted more extensively by Allardyce Nicoll in *A History of English Drama, 1660–1900* (Cambridge: Cambridge University Press, 1955), IV, 42–43.

fects. An effort was made to provide sets that actually resembled, rather than simply suggested, what they represented; and only during the second half of the nineteenth century did the box set, universally used today, come into being, with its illusion that we are looking through the fourth wall of a room. At the same time, the notion first gained acceptance that costumes should be roughly appropriate for the time and place represented in the play.

The net effect of this emphasis on visual authenticity was to throw into bold relief the unreal behavior of the characters in a play as well as the grossly artificial techniques of the actors. As a result, at the end of the century several playwrights sprang up, in various European countries, who were determined to return drama to reality, to give their characters believable motivation, and to allow them to face genuine human problems in a convincing way. To accommodate this new drama, independent and progressive theaters experimented not only with elaborately realistic sets but also with entirely new theories of acting, which encouraged actors to forget the old traditions of rhetoric and "voice projection" and not only to act but to *feel* like the characters they played.

The ideals of nineteenth-century realism were stated as early as 1881 by the French novelist Emile Zola:

> I am waiting for someone to put a man of flesh and bones on the stage, taken from reality, scientifically analyzed, and described without one lie. . . . I am waiting for environment to determine the characters, and the characters to act according to the logic of facts combined with the logic of their own disposition.[2]

The goal was achieved in the ruthless realism of Zola's own *Thérèse Raquin* (1873), about which he said:

> Given a strong man and an unsatisfied woman, to seek in them the beast, to see nothing but the beast, to throw them into a

[2] Émile Zola, "Le Naturalisme au théâtre," in *Playwrights on Playwriting,* ed. Toby Cole (New York: Hill & Wang, Inc., 1960), p. 6.

The Meaning of "Reality" in Drama

violent drama and note scrupulously the sensations and acts of these creatures. . . . I have simply done on two living bodies the work which surgeons do on corpses.[3]

Works of equal honesty and scientific objectivity, but of somewhat less brutality, were also produced at the "Free Theatres" in Paris and Berlin and at the great Moscow Art Theatre and have ultimately won acceptance in all the major theaters of the Western world.

The fight against dead conventions and formulas and falsity was not, and is not, an easy one; but today we take realism for granted, and without question it is the dominant tradition of the twentieth century. The possibilities for reproducing reality accurately have, of course, been tremendously enlarged by the art of photography, and the whole vogue of realism has been given impetus by the development of the movies and, more recently, of television. Producers and stage designers, as well as playwrights, have risen to the demands of photographic accuracy, and since the Moscow Art Theatre production of Gorki's *Lower Depths* in 1902 audiences have become accustomed to plays peopled by unshaven men in sweaty T-shirts, with real dirt under their fingernails, living in squalid slums with real dust on the floors.

Of such direct and sometimes brutal attempts to represent the less pleasant aspects of modern life the initial effect has usually been one of shock; and, on the whole, realism has been used to best advantage when employed for its shock value. Henrik Ibsen, the great Norwegian playwright of the late nineteenth century who is generally credited with being the "father" of modern realism, developed that particular technique as part of his effort to jolt his audiences out of the smugly complacent image of man and society that had been encouraged by the glib and superficial "well-made plays" of his day. Ibsen was not a crusader in the sense that he was pleading for a specific program of reform, but he did want to make his contemporaries face more honestly the

[3] Quoted in John Gassner, *Masters of the Drama* (New York: Random House, Inc., 1954), p. 400.

The Nature and Kinds of "Reality" in Drama

realities of their private and social morality; and realism was his
weapon. Later dramatists have used realism for frankly propa-
gandistic purposes; and from Gerhart Hauptmann's grim portrayal of economically depressed workers in *The Weavers* (1892)
through the plays of "social protest" of the depression years, the
realistic representation of poverty and crime on the stage has
been one means of bringing to the attention of the public the need
for economic or political reforms.

Realism, where it is used for a particular purpose, can be a
powerfully effective dramatic technique. It also has its limitations,
however. While it has value as a kind of shock treatment to jar
its audience into a truer understanding of themselves or of social
conditions, its effectiveness depends heavily on its novelty. The
nerves of an audience can easily become dulled from over-
exposure to sordidness and brutality; and too often playwrights
seem impelled to devote more attention to titillating their audience's jaded sensibilities with new extravagance in language and
situation than to bringing out the significance of the "reality"
they are trying to portray. The great danger of realism is that it
tends to become an end in itself rather than only a means to
an end.

Especially when realism was still a theatrical novelty, playwrights, directors, and audiences alike too often became fascinated by the real teakettle boiling on a real stove, the real
obscenities, the real tawdriness of everyday life, and forgot that
the "truth" of the boiling teakettle was no proof of the truth and
validity of the insights of the play as a whole. Much of the effectiveness of photography derives from the principle that seeing is
believing; a picture is true and convincing because we see an
object or scene in all its uniqueness and detail. In much the same
way, realism, as a dramatic technique, attempts to convince by
its visual authenticity. The difference is that a play *cannot* be the
"thing itself," and we, the audience, know it; we are never for a
moment deluded into confusing the pretense with the reality.
Even in the movies, with all their hypnotic persuasiveness, we
do not actually believe that our favorite star is in fact a truck

The Meaning of "Reality" in Drama

42   driver, especially since we saw him as a submarine captain last week and as a Wall Street tycoon the week before. And at a dramatic performance deception is even less possible. As we sit in an overheated theater, surrounded by hundreds of our fellow citizens—most of whom come late and climb over our cringing feet—with a program in our hand and on our lap a coat we wish we had left in the checkroom, no amount of subterfuge could convince us that we have accidentally wandered into a suburban bedroom, say, or a Dublin tenement.

Realism on the stage, in other words, is relative at best, and the most realistic production possible still demands considerable concession to unreality. Stage reality depends upon what we expect, or, to put it another way, must stay within the limits of what we are willing to accept. We are, on the whole, only too willing to make generous concessions to the fact that a play *is* a play, an illusion, and we do not insist that it literally fool us into thinking we are actually witnessing the events represented. We are quite ready to fill in with our imaginations as long as the playwright makes it clear just *what* we are to imagine.

The sum total of the concessions we are willing to make to unreality constitutes the *conventions* of the theater. Conventions might be described as unwritten agreements between the playwright—or, in a larger sense, the whole dramatic tradition of a given age—and the audience to allow certain things to "stand for" reality; the dramatist, in other words, requires of his audience the habit of accepting various modifications of, or short cuts to, literal truth. The stage itself is a convention, as is the custom of allowing actors to represent persons they obviously are not. Stage settings depend heavily on convention: We are able to accept a few papier-mâché trees and a painted backdrop as a forest without also insisting on grass and wildflowers, to say nothing of assorted insects. Even more demanding is the set consisting of a few pillars and a Gothic arch, which we will believe is an English cathedral or a Venetian palace or an Egyptian tomb, if the playwright will let us know which. Once we have made the initial concession of entering the theater—and it is no small concession—we will accept almost anything, so long as we are familiar with the convention, so long as we know how to fill in the gap between the pretense and the reality it represents.

Conventions change from age to age, however, and it is often difficult for one century to accept the conventions of another. If we are unfamiliar with the Elizabethan stage, the prospect of a character speaking loudly and rhetorically to himself may strike us as incredible and foolish, at least until we learn that the soliloquy is a device for making a person's inner thoughts known to the audience. The poetic language and the verse form of most of Shakespeare's plays are sometimes even more difficult for a twentieth-century audience to accept, seeming too far from the actual language of men even to approximate reality; yet how much more suggestive, how much more indicative of states of mind and depths of feeling, how much more revealing of the real man is Shakespeare's language than the often thin and utilitarian speech of the realistic theater. In point of fact, a careful comparison of the dialogue of a realistic play with the fragmentary, erratic, chaotic conversation of actual people will suggest that the language of the modern stage is not very much closer to authentic human speech than was Shakespeare's. The real difference is only one of degree; the significant difference for us is that one convention is familiar and the other is not.

Much the same can be said about the distinctions between realistic and nonrealistic drama: The difference is one of degree. Realism in the theater, for all its visual authenticity, is still a long way from being what it pretends to be; it still depends on what the audience is willing to pretend is real. Both realism and nonrealism, in other words, depend on conventions for their acceptance. One can, however, ask whether the photographic accuracy of realism is in fact an asset, or whether it may be possible that one of the unique virtues of the theater is that it doesn't *have* to limit itself to a literal reproduction of reality.

To illustrate the implications of this question, we might consider a somewhat debased art form that is vaguely dramatic, the comic strip. In most strips neither the characters nor the world

The Meaning of "Reality" in Drama

they live in bear more than the faintest possible physical resemblance to the real world—and we certainly do not communicate through little balloons filled with words. But such gross distortions do not bother us, because we simply are not looking for visual accuracy. All we ask is that the figures reveal, in what they say or in the situations they get themselves into, enough human characteristics and follies and foibles that we can take an interest in them, or through them laugh at human nature. We can, in other words, take the "art" of the comic strip in its own terms; it need be just real enough to serve its own particular purpose, a purpose that has nothing whatever to do with literal verisimilitude.

Drama, too, is frequently concerned with a reality that has nothing to do with appearances. Realism is simply *one* theatrical convention that can be used to convince us that the play is dealing with reality. The greatest danger of this technique is that it too often rests on the assumption that because something is authentic it is important. Unfortunately, it is easier to worry about realistic details than about whether the story is worth telling in the first place. It is, in other words, easier to take a picture than to paint one.

The snapshot, in taking in everything, frequently takes in too much. In painting, the artist leaves out some things and emphasizes others; he distorts reality in order to focus attention and to produce a certain effect. The object of portrait painting, for instance, is not merely to reproduce a face but also to bring out what is not always visible, the subject's personality. The art can be said to rest on the assumption that the uniqueness of any person lies not simply in appearance but in unseen qualities behind the surface. So too, much drama is based on the notion that the important aspects of human life and experience lie behind appearances, that portrayal of life in its raw form is senseless, and that the job of the playwright is to select and distort in order to focus on, and bring out, the reality *he* thinks is significant.

Another way to describe the relationship of realistic and nonrealistic drama to reality might be to use Hamlet's much-quoted metaphor of "holding a mirror up to nature"—although of course

The Nature and Kinds of "Reality" in Drama

he was referring to the art of acting, not playwriting. Realism might be compared to an inexpensive dime-store mirror, full of small, random, and unintentional distortions but pretending to give an accurate reflection. Nonrealistic drama, on the other hand, is like one of the mirrors in the fun house at an amusement park: It is intentionally distorted in order to create a specific effect.

Some Reactions Against Realism: Expressionism

Almost at the same time that some dramatists, such as Ibsen and Zola, were espousing the cause of realism, others were already dissatisfied with its limitations and its emphasis on surfaces; and most dramatists since that time can be divided roughly into two groups, comparable to our mirrors. Some hold as a dramatic ideal the accurate reproduction or representation of life; others, like the cartoonist, accept the fact that drama by the very nature of the medium involves distortion and use that distortion to create a special kind of world, in which some kinds of reality, such as accuracy of setting or language, may be sacrificed in order to enhance another, equally valid reality.

Although the several varieties of "reality" can be said to exist simultaneously, each can be viewed only from a particular point of view, and the playwright will often find the representations of different levels of reality mutually exclusive. Thus, he must some-times ignore one aspect of reality or bypass it through the use of conventions in order to give free scope to another aspect that seems, for the purposes of a particular play, more important.

The desire to present directly on the stage a perspective of reality other than the visual and literal has led to the experimenta-tion that is characteristic of the theater in the twentieth century. Ibsen and the realists successfully discredited many of the stale conventions of the nineteenth-century stage; and doubtless many

The Meaning of "Reality" in Drama

features of the popular melodramas and the "well-made plays" of the period deserved to die. In a sense, however, the baby may have been thrown out with the bath water. For better or worse, the twentieth-century dramatists who have rejected the limitations of "pure" realism have to a great extent been forced to create their own conventions, being no longer able to rely on those of a solidly established and generally understood tradition. This search for new techniques, as well as the disregard for the traditional categories or "modes" mentioned earlier, has made for chaos, extravagance, and misunderstanding; but it has also made for vitality, growth, and above all, an awareness that little can be taken for granted.

What has led so many modern playwrights to use various non-realistic techniques? Perhaps the principal consideration is the desire to represent concretely and vividly the psychological complexities of their characters. While it is true that a strictly realistic play can be psychologically authentic, in the sense that it does not violate our expectations regarding human behavior, the fact remains that neither in the real world nor on a realistic stage do words and actions by themselves fully reveal a person's true motives or actual thoughts. Drama has always been concerned with the "real" man; but with the development of the science of psychology and our awareness of the complex and often unconscious forces behind the simplest act, the dramatist has been forced to strain his ingenuity in order to get that reality onto the stage.

Take, for example, Arthur Miller's *Death of a Salesman* (1949).[1] In many respects, this work is solidly in the realistic tradition. The financial and emotional problems of a conspicuously "average" middle-class family, living in the somewhat run-down section of a big city, are characteristic grist for the realist's mill. The language of the play generally approximates that spoken by people of the class and educational level represented, and the actions and behavior of the characters are such as might reasonably be found in the world outside the theater. The set of the play is also representational, for, although the Loman house is shown

[1] In *Four Modern Plays,* pp. 239–338.

The Nature and Kinds of "Reality" in Drama

as transparent, it contains real beds, chairs, a refrigerator, and
so on. It is in the setting, however, that we first notice Miller's
attempt to suggest rather than show, to represent inner as well as
outer realities.

The description of the set begins, significantly, not with what
we see but with what we hear: *"A melody is heard, played upon
a flute. It is small and fine, telling of grass and trees and the
horizon."* Miller continues:

> Before us is the Salesman's house. We are aware of towering,
> angular shapes behind it, surrounding it on all sides. Only the
> blue light of the sky falls upon the house and forestage; the
> surrounding area shows an angry glow of orange. As more light
> appears, we see a solid vault of apartment houses around the
> small, fragile-seeming home.

Willy's house is largely transparent, in part so that the hard,
"angry," somewhat sinister presence of the surrounding apartment houses will always be before our eyes and our minds.
Throughout the play, we are reminded of the feeling of claustro-
phobia created by the towering walls of concrete and steel. On
several occasions, Willy complains bitterly that the encroaching
city has destroyed the trees and crowded out the sunlight, so that
his vegetables and flowers will no longer grow, and he and Linda
reminisce about the days when their home was "like being a
million miles from the city." At the end of Act II, when Willy
has reached the end of his rope, he is seen desperately planting
seeds in the hard, sterile soil; and the play ends with the stage
direction: *"Only the music of the flute is left on the darkening
stage as over the house the hard towers of the apartment buildings
rise into sharp focus."*

Miller uses the setting to symbolize both the objective fact and
a subjective point of view. On the one hand, the harsh, indifferent
city is slowly crushing all natural, spontaneous growth within it,
just as—or so Willy complains—the pressures and impersonality
of modern business are crushing the human and personal element.
Even more important, however, is Willy's attitude toward the
asphalt jungle he has chosen to conquer. Willy's conscious goals,

for himself and for his sons, are limited on one side by his image of Uncle Ben, who "went into the jungle at twenty-one and when he came out, by God he was rich," and on the other by his memories of Dave Singleman, who was "able to go, at the age of eighty-four, into twenty or thirty different cities, and pick up a phone, and be remembered and loved and helped by so many different people." But as Biff, who is the only major figure in the play to arrive at any kind of understanding, says, "He had the wrong dreams." The ideals of success and popularity, the Great American Dream, have been the moving forces in Willy's life; but beneath his self-delusion he is a simple, gentle, creative individual. Biff makes explicit a truth his father cannot see: "We don't belong in this nuthouse of a city! We should be mixing cement on some open plain, or—or carpenters. A carpenter is allowed to whistle!" Almost the final comment on Willy Loman at the end of the "Requiem" is: "There's more of him in that front stoop than in all the sales he ever made." "Yeah. He was a happy man with a batch of cement."

Willy is fighting against the current of his nature and is trying to force himself and his sons into an uncongenial mold; but he is unaware of this basic antipathy, and so he can never put it into words. The setting, then, with its implacable, ominous apartments seemingly crushing the fragile, withering house beneath them, is a kind of external representation of Willy's basic but uncomprehended incompatibility with the business world of the city, and at the same time it is a symbolic suggestion of what has happened, and is happening, to him.

A different and more dynamic means of revealing the subconscious is provided by Miller's use of the "flashback" technique. At the end of his initial stage direction the playwright says:

> *Before the house lies an apron, curving beyond the forestage into the orchestra. This forward area serves as the back yard as well as the locale of all Willy's imaginings. . . . Whenever the action is in the present the actors observe the imaginary wall-lines, entering the house only through its door at the left.*

But in the scenes of the past these boundaries are broken, and   49
characters enter or leave a room by stepping "through" a wall
onto the forestage.

Using such signals to the audience as are suggested here, and
with the help of lighting and music, Miller is able to probe into
Willy's mind, presenting directly on the stage his memories and
"visions," thereby leading us, if not Willy, to an understanding of
what makes him tick, of what the factors are that have made him
and his sons failures.

It is possible to find other basically unrealistic devices in the
play; but all of them—the musical motifs, the visions, the setting
—are used to represent directly and visually what supposedly lies
beneath the surface of consciousness and cannot be seen. This
style of dramatic writing, which attempts thus to project onto the
stage internal or subconscious or symbolic reality, is commonly
called "expressionism," a method that may be defined as the
significant distortion of reality in order to represent a particular
and personal point of view.

A somewhat different distortion of reality is employed by
Eugene O'Neill in *The Emperor Jones* (1920), but again its
function is to peel away the layers of conscious thought and to
probe the inner nature of the mind—in this case not merely of
the individual but of Man. In *The Emperor Jones,* O'Neill is not
interested, as was Miller, in exploring by means of visionary ex-
cursions into a personal past the sources of present behavior and
family relationships. Rather, he is tracing the reversion to a
primitive state of a human being under the pressure of a powerful
primitive emotion. For this reason, O'Neill's representations of a
psychological event are not significant for their narrative content,
as Miller's are in *Death of a Salesman,* but rather for their symbolic value. He puts on the stage the history of a subconscious
process that might, in slightly different terms, be experienced by
any man. Although the mind O'Neill chooses to investigate is that
of a Negro, he is not interested in the Negro race as such. It is
simply that the Negro's history from savagery to civilization has

been tremendously foreshortened and is therefore easier to trace within the limits of a play.

The initial point of view of *The Emperor Jones,* like that of *Death of a Salesman,* is realistic. The play is set in a small Caribbean kingdom tyrannized over by a shrewd and arrogant emperor, the former Pullman-car porter and escaped convict Brutus Jones. As long as Jones is in control of the situation, the frame of reference, as seen in language, setting, and action, is that of a recognizable "external" world, albeit an unfamiliar one. Jones's self-confidence in his control over the "real" world of ignorant natives and bootlicking traders is based on a supreme faith in his own intellectual and spiritual superiority, a superiority achieved, he freely admits, thanks to his contacts with "white folks" back in the States.

> If dey's one thing I learns in ten years on de Pullman ca's listenin' to de white quality talk, it's dat . . . dere's little stealin' like you does, and dere's big stealin' like I does. For de little stealin' dey gets you in jail soon or late. For de big stealin' dey makes you Emperor and puts you in de Hall o' Fame when you croaks.[2]

He is proud of the fact that he has exploited his "people" through sheer "Yankee bluff": "Ain't a man's talkin' big what makes him big?" And if the big talk fails, he always has his religion: "Doesn't you know dey's got to do wid a man was member in good standin' o' de Baptist Church. . . . De Baptist Church done pertect me and land dem all in hell." As final insurance, he adds, he always has his silver bullet: "She's my rabbit's foot."

Jones, in other words, sees himself as an embodiment of the achievements of civilization, wringing what is little more than his due from a primitive, uneducated, superstitious people. As he confesses to Smithers, his advantages are such that everything is almost too easy. O'Neill, too, sees the situation as a confrontation of civilization and savagery; but he is far less confident of the outcome.

Even Jones, however, recognizes that the most successful ex-

[2] In *Four Modern Plays,* pp. 207–236.

The Nature and Kinds of "Reality" in Drama

ploiter must reach the point where his victims have nothing left to give up but their lives and will rise against him; and he has prepared for this, too, by depositing his loot in foreign banks and hiding provisions along an escape route through the Great Forest. Brutus Jones has, in a word, everything accounted necessary to success: shrewdness, both in business and in handling people; nerve; wealth; a religion to salve his conscience; and an "escape route" if well-laid plans go awry. But there are more things in heaven and earth than are dreamt of in Jones's philosophy. Once he has got into the Great Forest and lost his way, once he has lost his grip on the solid world of gullible and obsequious natives, of gold, of well-laid plans, the inner flaws show up, and the whole empty shell collapses. As long as he is in a situation characteristic of "civilization," Jones can apply the civilized virtues of the "white quality" successfully; but, plunged into the wholly primitive, almost primordial world of the Great Forest, haunted by brute fear—represented by the ever-closer tom-toms—Jones discovers that his education has cost him those native instincts which, a generation or so before, would have saved him. Rushing blindly through the Forest in what turns out to be a circle, Jones is unable to fall back on that primitive knowledge that man once found in his closeness to nature; and at the same time those qualities and achievements he is so proud of—by which man has marked his slow and painful rise from the savage—he sees gradually fall from him like his useless and awkward clothing. In fact, O'Neill's device of suggesting that the Great Forest, scene by scene, strips off the Emperor's absurdly pretentious uniform, until he is left with only a loin cloth, is only a symbolic equivalent, in essentially realistic and "external" terms, of the inner process represented nonrealistically and expressionistically by the "visions."

In six brief episodes we witness Jones's reversion, in mind if not in literal fact, to his primitive and aboriginal state. The regression is traced through a series of apparitions that appear to Jones, figments conjured up out of his own mind by the elemental terror of his situation, and yet not to be viewed as conscious

The Meaning of "Reality" in Drama

memories. Of the five specific visions—not counting the "Little Formless Fears" of Scene ii—only the first two are from Jones's own past; the remainder, the slave block, the slave ship, and the Congo witch doctor, arise from the depths of his subconscious, from what Jung would call the "racial memory."

In the end it is not really Old Lem and the natives who destroy the once-proud Emperor but Jones himself, or rather that inner nature that no façade of civilization can wholly hide or suppress. And if, in terms of the literal action of the play, the natives are the principal agents of Jones's self-destruction, they are so because they are still in a state of instinctive oneness with nature and have not yet forgotten the elemental springs of human impulse. However, the heart of both the meaning and the impact of the play—and these are really the same thing—lies in the visions, ghostly specters of a suppressed inward nature that civilized man would like to ignore, can usually forget, but, O'Neill suggests, can never escape.

Nothing could be more "unreal" than this projection of visions onto the stage; yet within the context of the play, Jones's "real" world of gold and ignorant savages and personal success turns out to be far less real than the unconscious inner world represented by the apparitions. It is just this subconscious, or at least unseen, level of reality that expressionism is designed to explore. A more extreme example of the method can be found, however, in the works of the man who to a great extent originated this concept of dramatic representation, August Strindberg.

Strindberg, writing in Sweden at the end of the nineteenth century, had produced several first-rate plays in the realistic mode with which Ibsen had already pioneered, although he was perhaps even more rigorously "scientific" than Ibsen in his treatment of environment and heredity. His restless and original mind apparently found the limitations of realism galling, however, and after the turn of the century he wrote a series of plays in which he violated almost all the established conventions of the theater in order to create a language by which he might project onto the stage his own highly personal and perhaps unbalanced view of

The Nature and Kinds of "Reality" in Drama

reality. Whereas the expressionistic experiments of Miller and O'Neill have at least one foot solidly in the realistic tradition, Strindberg's are from beginning to end wholly divorced from the everyday world as we see it around us. The angle of distortion, one might say, is constant.

The world of Strindberg's expressionistic plays is the dream world, in which the subconscious has free play and psychological "reality" appears in symbolic form. Perhaps the best possible description of his technique is in the Author's Note attached to *A Dream Play* (1902), where Strindberg says he has

> sought to reproduce the disconnected but apparently logical form of a dream. Anything can happen; everything is possible and probable. Time and space do not exist; on a slight ground-work of reality, imagination spins and weaves new patterns made up of memories, experiences, unfettered fancies, absurdities and improvisations.
>
> The characters are split, double and multiply; they evaporate, crystallize, scatter and converge. But a single consciousness holds sway over them all—that of the dreamer. For him there are no secrets, no incongruities, no scruples and no law. He neither condemns nor acquits, but only relates . . . .[3]

It is not entirely clear whether we are to imagine the dreamer, the unifying consciousness of the play, to be the Daughter of Indra, the only figure who appears in all its episodes; or perhaps Strindberg himself; or, on another level, each individual who sees or reads the play. Certain it is that at some point or another the play has touched a responsive chord in a large number of people. And Strindberg's success in achieving this response is not necessarily dependent on the intellectual content or "message" of the play: his peculiarly pessimistic view that life is inherently a condition of suffering and disappointment, that all happiness is paid for thrice over by pain, and that regret and disillusionment are the only things we can be sure of. The special virtue of Strindberg's technique is that it bypasses the rational judgment. It is the form that is convincing, not what we consciously see and hear; and, while

[3]In *Playwrights on Playwriting*, pp. 182–183, or prefaced to most editions of the play.

our intellect may rebel, there is in us an instinct, born of a hundred half-remembered dreams, that tells us that this is indeed the way the subconscious works. All Strindberg's dream plays are in this sense "unintelligible," and it takes an almost conscious act of will to overcome, as one must in order to understand them, all the prejudices and habits of mind bred by our heritage of realistic and logical plays.

 **Fantasy**

Strindberg's influence on the development of modern drama, while not so broad as that of Ibsen, has probably been equally important. Although the technique of expressionism has rarely been carried to the extreme of *A Dream Play,* unless in the plays of the German expressionists Ernst Toller and Georg Kaiser following World War I, it has proved a fruitful language of the theater for some of the most important playwrights of the twentieth century. We should not suppose, however, that any play employing fantasy or symbolism or any other obviously unrealistic technique is necessarily expressionistic. Expressionism, because it involves a distortion of reality, could be called a kind of fantasy; but the distortions of fantasy need not reflect a specific point of view nor represent the workings of a particular subconscious mind, as is normally the case with expressionism. Indeed, fantasy frequently treats reality far more loosely than expressionism does and with a very different end in view.

Thornton Wilder's *Skin of Our Teeth* (1942) is fantasy, and about as far removed from observable reality as one can get; yet the direction his unrealism takes is diametrically opposed to that of Strindberg in *A Dream Play.* The structure and effect of Strindberg's play depend on the subconscious, associative movements of the mind and the relationships between the various symbols and figures—say, the growing castle and the eternally pasteing

Kristin and the world of Fairhaven and Foulstrand—cannot be reduced to any explicit statement or clear-cut formula without destroying the very essence of the dramatic experience. Wilder's distortions, on the other hand, are not subjective and do not represent an effort to project on the stage a specific state of mind, as O'Neill's and Miller's did. They are, rather, objective and rational, imposed as it were from the outside and responded to by the intellect.

It is perfectly true that the words of Strindberg's preface to *A Dream Play* could be applied appropriately to *The Skin of Our Teeth:* "Anything can happen. . . . Time and space do not exist. . . . The characters are split, double and multiply." The play opens in what is ostensibly the suburban New Jersey home of Mr. and Mrs. Antrobus, but even before the end of the introductory "newsreel" it is apparent that Mr. Antrobus is no ordinary suburbanite. He is that, but he is also Adam (his son Henry's real name is Cain, and the telegram to his wife is addressed to Eva); he is a creature of the Ice Age (the glaciers are advancing over Boston and Hartford); the inventor of the wheel, the alphabet, and the multiplication table; and a patron of the arts (he would save Homer, Moses, the Muses, and the works of Shakespeare from destruction). In other words, even if we failed to recognize the significance of his name, a thinly disguised distortion of the Greek word for man, it would be apparent that Mr. Antrobus represented a kind of composite "Everyman," comprehending in one figure the history of the race from the beginning to the present. Or perhaps it would be more accurate to say that he stands for one side of man's nature, the imaginative, creative, idealistic element that has brought us up from the slime and has carried us through a thousand natural and man-made disasters "by the skin of our teeth." He is the humanizing and civilizing impulse that has always opposed the forces of despair and chaos and has found in the wreckage of one civilization that with which to create another and perhaps better one. But Wilder is enough of a realist to know that man, even at his best, is not perfect, and

The Meaning of "Reality" in Drama

Mr. Antrobus is represented as being often blind and often something of a fool. He is, in a word, what Pope called "the glory, jest, and riddle of the world."

Even so, Mr. Antrobus does not represent the whole story of man's nature. There is another side, epitomized by Henry (or Cain), with the mark of the murderer on his forehead. He is the antisocial element in man, the malcontent, the rebel against society's restrictions; unloved and unloving, he is the world's eternal juvenile delinquent. To assert his own individuality and independence, he would destroy all that the Antrobuses have created, and in Act III he almost does. The play ends, however, on a note of hope. In his three loves—for man, for his wife and children, and for the ideas stored in books—Mr. Antrobus finds the will and the strength to begin again.

Wilder's characterization of the women in the play follows much the same somewhat mechanical division. Mrs. Antrobus seems to represent the domestic impulse in womanhood. Her ruling instinct is the survival of the family; as Sabina says of her: "If it would be any benefit to her children she'd see the rest of us stretched out dead at her feet,"[1] and later in Act I she only reluctantly, and at Mr. Antrobus' insistence, shares her family's dwindling supply of heat and food with the refugees, Homer, Moses, and the Muses. Like her husband, she is often foolish, largely because of the narrowness of her intellectual horizons; but she has a sure instinct for survival, and while Antrobus is off saving civilization she is perpetuating the species and the family. If Mrs. Antrobus is the eternal mother, Lily-Sabina is the eternal feminine—seductive, pleasure-seeking, and selfish. She is not positively dangerous or destructive in the sense that Henry is, but she is a kind of dead weight that humanity must carry with it on its journey; she stands for all those who can see no further than their own immediate amusement, who are unwilling to face the pain and self-denial that the struggle upward entails, who are

---

[1] The quotations from *The Skin of Our Teeth* are from *Contemporary Drama: Fifteen Plays,* ed. E. Bradlee Watson and Benfield Pressey (New York: Charles Scribner's Sons, 1959), pp. 423–452.

If Wilder had made these arbitrary divisions of character traits in order to emphasize and dramatize the consciousness that could make such a division, as O'Neill or Strindberg construct their "dreams" so as to illuminate the mind of the dreamer, *The Skin of Our Teeth* might fairly be called expressionistic. But Wilder is not particularly concerned with either his own or any other particular mind. He takes it for granted that his representation of human nature is roughly analogous to observable fact, and his manipulation of the symbolic figures is his rational comment on the durability and future of humanity. And when the play first appeared, during World War II, it sounded a refreshing note of hope at a time when the Henrys of the world were dangerously close to having it all their own way.

The appeal of *The Skin of Our Teeth* lies both in the kind of comment Wilder has to make and in the manner in which he makes it. Certainly, much of the success of the play results from its humor, a kind of humor that depends heavily on the fact that the audience is aware of what is "going on." Some of the fun arises from the sheer incongruity of the situations that Wilder's technique permits: shooing dinosaurs off the front lawn of a suburban home, or having the announcement of the discovery that ten tens make a hundred delivered as part of a singing telegram. Even more basic, however, is the mild irony the playwright can derive from the audience's recognition of Mr. Antrobus' multiple identity, as revealed in the statement that "he was once a gardener, but left that situation under circumstances that have been variously reported," or in the storm warnings in Act II. By the same token, if we do not catch the allusions to the Garden of Eden or the Flood, we miss both the humor and the point of the play.

Wilder, in other words, is appealing directly to our conscious intellects, to an at least superficial knowledge of history and the Old Testament, and to our ability to decipher precisely what kind of game he is playing with reality. And it is a kind of game. This is not the projection of man's subconscious; it is not even a significant distortion of reality; it is something we are given *instead* of reality. Indeed, Wilder goes out of his way to insist on the unreality of his stage action. On several occasions, at least once in each act, he has one or more of his characters drop their roles in the play and address the audience directly, as when Sabina wails in Act I: "I hate this play and every word in it. . . . I don't understand a single word of it anyway. . . . I'll say the lines, but I won't think about the play. And I advise *you* not to think about it either." This device is undoubtedly a source of humor but, more important, it is a forceful reminder to the playgoers that what they are watching makes no pretense of being reality and that they should not look at it as though it did. It is as though Wilder were to say: "This is not a piece of life I am showing you; this is a play. And my characters and situations are grotesque and fantastic, but they are at some few points analogous to their counterparts in the world of real men. All I ask is that you observe and understand the points of contact—and sit back and enjoy my telescoped history of the human race."

Grotesque as the play may be, *The Skin of Our Teeth* only does in an exaggerated way what almost all plays try to do: It emphasizes what is universal by minimizing what is particular, local, and exceptional. Indeed, since what is universal—or at least is true of a large number of people in different times and places—must in some sense of the word be "real," universality is the kind of reality that most drama tries to touch. Strindberg, by dramatizing the actual associative and symbolizing processes of the subconscious, makes what he intends to be a universal comment on the paradoxes of human nature and the tragedy of human experience. O'Neill and Miller are perhaps slightly more restricted in their points of view, in that they employ their explorations of the subconscious in order to make a comment on the split personality of specifically modern, "civilized" man. In *The Skin of Our Teeth,* Wilder does not rely on our instinctive recognition of the validity of his picture of the human mind or human experience. His appeal is more to our conscious minds; the argument of the play, and it is an argument, is essentially by analogy. He is saying that, since man, whether viewed by an anthropologist, by a historian, or through a literal interpretation of the Bible, has in the past always found the faith and the will to overcome the powers of despair and chaos, he will continue to do so now.

Thus, if the expressionist playwright tries to achieve reality by presenting a valid image of the processes of the human mind, most others do so by handling the more external events of human experience in such a way that the audience will see the conflicts and triumphs and failures of the stage world as *analogous* to situations in their own experience, and in that of all men. *The Skin of Our Teeth* is a little unusual in this respect, since it starts with an insistent assertion of the generalized statement from which we are to draw the particular conclusion, whereas in most cases the particular statement is made in such a way that we can make our own generalizations. But the difference is not really significant, since in either case the result is a dramatic experience involving the same basic idea: that what seems individual and isolated in human events, and therefore meaningless, is in fact part of a coherent whole, something common to the human condition.

One of the characteristics of realistic drama is that it necessarily places so much emphasis on the concrete, the particular, and the local that often the universal "realities" do not easily emerge above the photographic details. The realist might say that he too is striving for universality and that for the modern audience this goal can be reached more directly and more effectively through what is specific and physical—the illusion of reality—than through the suggestiveness of metaphor, symbol, and fantasy. The reasoning behind the strictly realistic play would seem to be that because the event portrayed *is* (we can actually see it happen), therefore it *could* be (that is, is universal). The dramatist who is not primarily concerned with the illusion of literal reality seems to operate in the opposite direction: Only

The Meaning of "Reality" in Drama

because an event or situation is true of human experience in general does he undertake to give it a more or less concrete dramatization.

Strindberg once complained of the realism "which includes everything, even the grain of dust on the lens of the camera, . . . the little art which does not see the forest for the trees, . . . the misunderstood naturalism which holds that art merely consists of drawing a piece of nature in a natural way."[2] Nonrealistic playwrights—and even some who are essentially within the realistic tradition—have been aware of the dangers of relying too heavily on mere verisimilitude, and most of the nonrealistic techniques and experiments of the modern stage represent the efforts of these playwrights to underline the universal implications of whatever specific events and situations they put before our eyes.

In another play by Thornton Wilder, *Our Town* (1938), the setting is highly specific in terms of time and place; yet by its extreme simplicity—for he gives us little more than the outline of a plot—this unpretentious tale of adolescent love and of marriage and death generates a powerful sense that it could have happened in any age and any country. Wilder also employs a kind of obvious theatricality akin to that of *The Skin of Our Teeth*. The stage is almost completely bare, except for a few crude props that serve only to emphasize the absence of a more elaborate set; and the details of the setting, as well as several chronological leaps, are filled in by a stage manager who spends nearly half the play "chatting" with the audience. Once again, the playwright is deliberately turning the audience's attention away from particular, realistic details in order to focus it on the universal aspects of his story.

"History" Plays

While Wilder's objectives are typical of most playwrights who use nonrealistic techniques, his methods are perhaps too extreme

[2] "On Modern Drama and Modern Theatre," in *Playwrights on Playwriting*, p. 17.

to be truly representative. There are other ways, however, in which a dramatist can create the conviction of universality by making us feel that, whereas the situation he is portraying may not be the *same* as one we might ourselves experience, it is at least analogous to one that could be real for us or for any human. One effective device for suggesting such expanding analogies is to place the story some distance in the past. If, in doing this, the playwright delineates the characters, the problems, and the conflicts in such a way that the similarities to contemporary situations and dilemmas are apparent, the sense that they represent universal phenomena can be almost inescapable.

Arthur Miller has used this technique in his historical play, *The Crucible* (1953), although in this instance the controversial nature of the analogy has led to some misunderstanding. Setting the play in colonial Salem at the time of its famous "witch-hunts," Miller drew some fairly obvious parallels with the hearings being conducted in the 1950's by Senator Joseph McCarthy of Wisconsin in an effort to uncover subversives in sensitive or responsible government positions. Whatever the merits or sincerity of the Senator's investigations, there is probably little doubt that his methods did encourage in some quarters the kind of hysterical and irresponsible accusations and "trial by public opinion" rather than by court of law that characterized the Salem witch trials. Whether in employing these parallels Miller was, as he has been accused of doing, using drama as a political weapon and making a thinly veiled attack on McCarthy is not really important. The play rises above the particular political situations involved, and it does so largely because the very existence of the parallel suggests that the situations and personal qualities involved are not limited to any particular historical era. We may take *The Crucible* as a comment on what happens when political leadership clothes itself in the robes of sanctity and thereby automatically discredits all opposition as coming from the agents of Hell, or as a comment on the dilemma of the individual conscience in conflict with public opinion, or on the struggles of an honest and conscientious man to overcome the disintegrating effects of guilt

62   —and all these are themes of the play. From whichever point of
view, the tragedy of John Proctor, the forces he defies, and the
values he defends are relevant to all men who exist as both individuals and social beings.

George Bernard Shaw achieves much the same effect in his
plays on historical subjects, although he usually employs his
parallels for satiric rather than tragic purposes. Shaw tends to
use two somewhat different kinds of universalizing analogies. He
cannot resist the temptation to take digs at various absurdities
of human nature, and so he peoples his "history" plays with
foolish, blind little people, who sometimes have very little to do
with the action but who are devastatingly familiar as our neigh-
bors, our friends, ourselves. On the broader level of the plays as
a whole the same universalizing process occurs, though often less
obviously. In *Saint Joan* (1924), for instance, the action of the
play appears to be closely tied to specific historical events, personalities, and problems. But the analogy is present. Certainly
the breakdown of the feudal system is no longer a burning social
issue, and the Catholic Church has long since lost its hold on a
large segment of mankind. And yet Shaw is at pains to suggest that
the central conflict of the play—the confrontation between institutions dedicated to defending and perpetuating the status quo and
a force representative of change and therefore of the future—is
as real today as it was in the fifteenth century. In case we have
missed the point, the playwright adds a little epilogue, in which
all the figures in the play are translated in a dream into the
twentieth century. Joan has just been officially canonized and
each representative of the forces that had betrayed her symbolically kneels to praise her and beg forgiveness. But when Joan,
encouraged by their adoration, offers to return to the world, they
are horrified, and each tactfully suggests that perhaps the world is
"better off" without its saints. The tragedy is not Joan's, but
Man's; and her final cry echoes down the vast expanse of human
history: "O God that madest this beautiful earth, when will it be
ready to receive Thy saints? How long, O Lord, how long?"

Historical plays, including Shaw's, are not usually much con-

The Nature and Kinds of "Reality" in Drama

cerned with accurate re-creation of either the events or the persons of the past. Indeed, the elements in the historical story that attract most playwrights are simply those that seem to have contemporary relevance—that is, those that are universal—and these may be slight indeed. Jean Anouilh's recent play *Becket* (1959) is a retelling of the historic conflict between Henry II of England and his Archbishop of Canterbury, Thomas à Becket, in terms that a true historian would view as sheerest fantasy. In his preface, Anouilh confesses that after he had written the play a historian pointed out to him that a fairly crucial point in the plot, that Becket was a Saxon, had been proved to be untrue fifty years ago. But, he says, it makes a better play the way it is, and so he made no change. The vital element in the play, the conflict between loyalty to spiritual and to temporal authority, remains intact; and, while Anouilh could perfectly well have told his story in modern terms, by putting it in a seemingly historical context he has in a sense forced us to make analogies that in turn suggest the universal relevance of his theme.

Placing the action of a play at a distance in time can thus have much the same effect as employing fantasy: that of de-emphasizing the importance or even the expectation of accuracy in details. The playwright's attitude usually seems to be that perhaps things did not happen in just this way, but they *could* have—and that, after all, is what is important. But if the distance of time serves to intensify the universal elements of a story placed in the past, should not the same be true of a play about the future? The relatively few serious plays that have been set in the future suggest that this is possible; but, while writing about the future may give broader scope to the playwright's unfettered imagination, it also places on him a heavier burden of responsibility. If the writer about the past fails to create characters or situations that are sufficiently convincing and universal, he can usually fall back on the excuse of historical accuracy and perhaps use authenticity as a device to hold our attention. But the writer about the future, once he has exhausted our curiosity about the marvels of a push-button, electronic, high-speed brave new world, has either to

The Meaning of "Reality" in Drama

convince us that his people and their problems are at least probable or to fall back on the sensationalism of third-rate science-fiction. He has, in other words, no mere facts to rely on to make his play believable.

Karel Čapek's famous play about the day when the robots take over the world is just such a work. *R.U.R.* (1921) bears, obviously, little relation to observable reality; yet the humans in the play reveal qualities so real, so true to human nature, that were the power they possess actually to exist, the development of the action, fantastic as it is, would seem perfectly logical. If we accept the premises that man can find meaning and purpose in life only through working and creating and that it is possible for an absolute substitute for human labor to be found, the working out of these premises in terms of believable personalities and situations makes the end of civilization on some distant Rossum's Island terrifyingly real.

VI Poetic Drama

It should not be supposed, however, that time alone can provide the kind of distance that may free the invention of the playwright or the attention of the audience from the details of everyday reality. Other techniques can serve to create a frame of reference wherein the audience will not *expect* to be shown a photographic likeness of life and human nature, thus liberating the imagination of the artist so that it may roam the world of fancy and find there the best means to express what in the depths of his soul he knows to be true and real. Poetry, because it is and always has been the language of imagination, has traditionally been the means by which a playwright takes his audience out of mundane reality into its own very special, but at the same time universal, world. The complaint sometimes made of a poetic play, that people simply do not speak that way, is completely beside the point. Of course they don't, and that is just why the playwright uses the device. To be sure, poetry can be effective in drama for many other reasons; but its most characteristic qualities, the almost subliminal surge and ebb of its rhythms, the suggestive richness of its figurative language, the heightened perceptions of its unusual word-orders, all serve to make our minds and our emotions more acutely responsive, more open to the conviction of universal truth, than is the case with any other technique.

Poetic drama in the literal sense of verse drama is a relative rarity on the modern stage, except in revivals of plays of an earlier tradition—Elizabethan, say, or Greek. But even apart from such experiments with versification as Maxwell Anderson's *Winterset* (1935), the twentieth century has produced its share of poetic drama. The plays of the Irishman John Millington Synge, of the Spaniard Federico Garcia Lorca, of the Frenchman Jean Giraudoux, or such American plays as *The Glass Menagerie* (1945) of Tennessee Williams qualify as poetic drama even without the use of verse. The rhythms, the imagery, the unrealistic language, to which might be added the poetic use of setting and lighting—in other words, all the characteristic intensifications of experience that we associate with poetry— can be used in drama that at least *visually* appears to be prose and can thereby make it poetic.

Tom Wingfield in *The Glass Menagerie* is a poet, and he speaks with the tongue of a poet. The narrative speeches with which he opens the play and several of the scenes, and with which he brings the drama to a close, are a long way from the language of ordinary men; and though the dialogue in the rest of the play more closely resembles that of everyday life, the poetic quality is sustained by the set, the lighting, and above all the mood. Williams announces at the beginning of the play the kind of "distance" he hopes to achieve, for it is a "memory play," the action being seen through the mind of Tom. In a sense, then, it is an expressionistic play. The subjective point of view, however, is maintained not by Strindberg's symbolic fantasies or by O'Neill's projected visions but by a sad, dim, nostalgic mood evoked by its poetry. Told in purely realistic terms, the play

The Meaning of "Reality" in Drama

would probably be unbearably sentimental. But because the story of Amanda and Laura is told through Tom's poeticizing memory, it becomes his play too; and its sentimentality seems justified because the pathos is in part a function of Tom's remorse. In the shadowy, half-remembered moods that the poetry evokes, the memories seem to become our own; and in the poetic introductions and epilogue with which Tom places the time of the action in terms of events in the outside world, the people and incidents of the play become like fragments floating somewhere in our own past. And so this sad and gently tragic story of three people who cannot face reality and of one who runs away becomes in a curious way an image of our own vague and inarticulate remorse at the failure of love to be strong enough to match responsibility.

It has been said before, but it is worth emphasizing, that the process by which poetry generalizes and universalizes the mood or implications of a play is not a logical one. Poetry does not show the way; it simply frees the mind and lets down the barriers to perceptions that are beyond, or perhaps below, the purely intellectual. This happens, even more powerfully, in Synge's *Riders to the Sea* (1904), one of the true masterpieces of modern poetic drama. The poetry of this basically realistic play comes from the playwright's handling of the colorful and highly figurative language of the Irish peasants on the Aran Islands. Its effect is to transmute a deceptively simple story into a moving statement about man's eternal relationship to the power of nature, the source of his life and his death. Perhaps "statement" is too strong a word, since nothing so concrete and rational is appropriate to the effect of the play. "Emotion" might be better; and that is, after all, the realm of poetry.

Poetry, in addition to employing rhythm and figurative language, also tends to treat reality, at whatever level, in symbolic terms; and *Riders to the Sea,* as a poetic play, has its share of symbols. The drowned son's clothes, the coffin boards, the sea itself, to mention only a few, all represent or suggest things outside and beyond themselves. It is sometimes claimed that the tendency of modern literature to express itself in symbolic terms is part of a movement away from the fundamental, the concrete, the intrinsic, and therefore the really important elements of human experience, toward the realm of intellectuality and abstraction. Whether such a process is taking place or not, its origin does not lie in the use of symbols. It is perfectly true that symbols point to something beyond themselves; they stand for something larger than the particular "thing" used as a symbol. But the process of generalization is not the same as that of abstraction. By letting the sea become a symbol for the pervasive power of nature, for its power to sustain life as well as destroy it, Synge does not reduce the sea to a mere abstract idea but makes it immensely more immediate and awesome than it could be as simply a large body of water. The extension from the particular instance to the more universal application, which is what symbolism strives for, can make something seem *more* concrete and fundamental rather than less. Anton Chekhov, to give another example, achieves much the same effect in his use of the cherry orchard as a symbol in the play of that name. Without it, the play would be a trivial tale of individual incompetence and failure. With it, and all the complex ways in which the characters' attitudes toward it identify both their own and the orchard's symbolic values, the play becomes a story of the end of an era and the passing of a way of life, and indeed a comment on the tragedy and comedy of all human beings caught in the flux of historical changes they only half perceive and control not at all.

VIII The Play of Ideas

There is another kind of play that may or may not employ symbols but that is quite frankly and openly concerned with abstractions. The writer of the "play of ideas," as it has come to be called, is concerned, however, with a quite different kind of reality than are the playwrights we have talked about so far. For him, at least within the limits of his play, the truly significant reality *is* the idea itself. Of course, the idea may, in the world outside the theater, be related also to real facts and problems. And within the play, the ideas may be embodied or represented by more or less realistic people. What is important to the playwright, however, is the idea itself and its relation to other ideas; and the supposedly human creatures of the play tend to become the shadowy representatives of philosophical positions.

The complaint is sometimes heard that this kind of play is by its very nature undramatic. But this is not so. George Bernard Shaw, one of the foremost exponents of the play of ideas, replied to the charge that his plays were all talk by admitting to it: "just as Raphael's pictures are all paint, Michael Angelo's statues all marble, Beethoven's symphonies all noise. . . . Without a stock of ideas, mind cannot operate and plays cannot exist. The quality of a play is the quality of its ideas."[1] This is perfectly true, although with typical overstatement Shaw ignores the fact that the ideas behind a play need not be explicitly stated. In a play of ideas, however, they do need to be explicit, and they usually are. There is no necessary reason, on the other hand, why the fortunes and failures of those ideas, and the conflicts between them, should not be just as dramatic as the conflicts between individuals. As Shaw has frequently pointed out, in human history ideas have often proved more important and more interesting than individuals.

Shaw's own characteristic technique is that of taking two ideas that he finds current and significant and that are diametrically opposed in some basic way, embodying them in specific characters in his play, and letting the ideas, rather than the individuals, fight it out. In *Major Barbara* (1905), for example, he sets Barbara's religion of passivity, acceptance, and love against Undershaft's religion of money, gunpowder, and the survival of the fittest. Shaw makes a strong case for both sides, and the conflict between these two ways of looking at the world

---

[1]"The Play of Ideas, *"The New Statesman and Nation,* XXXIX (May 6, 1950); reprinted in *Shaw on Theatre,* ed. E. J. West (New York: Hill & Wang, Inc., 1959), p. 290.

occupies most of the play. The resolution of the conflict, as is again characteristic of Shaw, is a kind of synthesis involving the best element in each philosophy: in this case, the dynamism of Undershaft's religion fused with the moral responsibility of Barbara's Christianity. But the outcome of the action and our response to it depend on our attitudes toward the characters as representatives of particular viewpoints rather than on our attitudes toward them as characters per se.

The ultimate abstraction from the concrete and the human is Shaw's "Don Juan in Hell" episode in *Man and Superman* (1905). This *is* nothing but talk in its purest form, nothing but a battle of ideas. The greatest proof that such a play can be dramatic is that this episode, read by actors seated behind reading stands, was a smash hit on Broadway and later toured the United States with resounding success.

One of the most brilliant—or at least dazzling—writers of the "play of ideas" was the Italian Luigi Pirandello. The most intellectually challenging of his plays explore in a whimsical but penetrating way the elusive question, "What *is* this abstraction we call reality?" His masterpiece along this line, a tour de force of intellectual juggling, is *Six Characters in Search of an Author* (1921). In this fascinating and annoying play, Pirandello juxtaposes various kinds of reality: that of the world of art, both as it exists in the artist's imagination and independently in the work itself, set against the concrete, everyday world; and that of human personality, caught and fixed in our own or other people's conception of what we *are,* set against man's true nature, which is constantly in a state of flux.

The basic situation of the play is characteristic of the unconventional devices Pirandello delights in using to stimulate the mental digestive juices of his audience. Six characters have been called into "reality" by the imagination of an artist but have been left suspended, unfulfilled and unresolved, when the playwright left the work unfinished; and the action of the play centers on their efforts to persuade a theater manager to give them the opportunity to act out their story and their "identities" to comple-

The Meaning of "Reality" in Drama

tion. Consequently, we are confronted from the very beginning with at least three kinds of reality—that of the real world of the audience, that of the Stage Manager and the Actors, and that of the unfinished play-within-a-play represented by the six characters. But this is only the beginning, and Pirandello manipulates and complicates the paradoxes of the situation with fantastic ingenuity. At one point the Father, one of the six characters, says to the Stage Manager:

> If we [the Characters] have no other reality beyond illusion, you too must not count overmuch on your reality as you feel it today, since, like that of yesterday, it may prove an illusion for you tomorrow. . . . Our reality doesn't change. . . . Ours is an immutable reality which should make you shudder when you approach us if you are really conscious of the fact that your reality is a mere transitory and fleeting illusion.[2]

And so it goes, until in the superb and hopelessly confusing ending we find ourselves, or rather the play, suspended somewhere between at least four levels of "reality." And, what is worse, we are not at all sure which is the most real.

Pirandello does not answer the question; nor is it, perhaps, capable of being answered. *Six Characters* is very close to a "pure" play of ideas, the modern theater's most self-conscious exploration of the questions with which we began the chapter. Since we have come full circle, and since this kind of self-conscious intellectuality tends to become a dramatic dead end, we might turn back for a while and consider ways in which reality has been handled in the drama of the past.

SUGGESTIONS FOR READING

For those who wish to explore further and to read other examples of the various types of plays discussed in this chapter, the

[2] *Six Characters in Search of an Author* (Act III), tr. Edward Storer, in *Modern Drama: Nine Plays*, ed. Otto Reinert (Boston: Little, Brown & Co., 1962), pp. 292-293.

suggestions below may be helpful. The plays mentioned are available, either individually or as part of collections, in inexpensive paperback editions.

Realistic plays can, up to a point, be divided into two groups. There are the plays, like those of Ibsen, in which realism is used as a weapon of social criticism and even reform, frequently called "problem plays." And there are those that strive to achieve Zola's ideal of scientific detachment and objectivity.

Of Ibsen's plays, probably *A Doll's House* (1879), *An Enemy of the People* (1882), and *Ghosts* (1881) best exemplify his treatment of contemporary social problems. Although Strindberg did not agree with Ibsen's particular social bias, some of his nonexpressionistic plays are very similar (see *The Father,* 1887, and *Miss Julie,* 1888). In the same tradition, in England, are the plays of John Galsworthy (see *Strife,* 1909, *Justice,* 1910), and the early work of George Bernard Shaw (*Mrs. Warren's Profession,* 1905, *Candida,* 1897). In America Ibsen's literary descendents are legion and would include some of O'Neill's realistic plays (*Desire Under the Elms,* 1924), most of the works of Sidney Howard (*The Silver Cord,* 1926), Lillian Hellman (*The Children's Hour,* 1934, *The Little Foxes,* 1939), William Inge (*Come Back, Little Sheba,* 1950), Arthur Miller (*All My Sons,* 1947), and a few plays by Tennessee Williams (*Streetcar Named Desire,* 1947).

In the scientific, naturalistic tradition begun by Zola, his own *Thérèse Raquin* (1873), Henry Becque's *The Vultures* (1882), and Maxim Gorki's *The Lower Depths* (1902) are the best examples. Chekhov, although writing with a gentler tone and a subtler technique, maintains much the same kind of sympathetic objectivity (*The Sea Gull,* 1898, *Uncle Vanya,* 1899, *The Three Sisters,* 1901). Inevitably, the naturalistic, "slice-of-life" play came to be used to expose distressing moral or social conditions, and it has become almost indistinguishable from the Ibsenesque problem play. Perhaps the first to take this direction was Gerhart Hauptmann's *The Weavers* (1892); in the same category we could include some of the works of Sean O'Casey (*Juno and the Paycock,* 1924), Sidney Kingsley (*Dead End,* 1935), Clifford Odets (*Waiting for Lefty,* 1935), and even O'Neill (*A Long Day's Journey Into Night,* 1956).

Plays employing the expressionistic techniques in which Strindberg pioneered include those by Georg Kaiser (*The Coral,* 1917, and especially *Gas I* and *II,* 1918 and 1920), Hauptmann (*Hannele,* 1893), Elmer Rice (*The Adding Machine,* 1923), and O'Neill (*The Hairy Ape,* 1922, *The Great God Brown,* 1926).

Further examples of plays set in the past in order to make a comment on the present are *Caesar and Cleopatra* (Shaw, 1901), *The Lark* and *Antigone* (Anouilh, 1958, 1944), *A Touch of the Poet* (O'Neill, 1958).

Fantasy has been used for a wide variety of purposes very different from that for which Wilder employs the device: See *The Infernal Machine* (Jean Cocteau, 1934), *Camino Real* (Tennessee Williams, 1953), *The Madwoman of Chaillot* (Jean Giraudoux, 1945), *The Green Pastures* (Marc Connelly, 1930), or *The Chairs* (Eugene Ionesco, 1952). A notable experiment that reverses the usual procedure by moving from fantasy to reality, rather than the reverse, as well as using poetry, is Archibald MacLeish's *J. B.* (1958).

Poetic drama is at best an ill-defined category, but its most noteworthy practitioners are J. M. Synge (*Playboy of the Western World,* 1907), Edmund Rostand (*Cyrano de Bergerac,* 1897), Federico Garcia Lorca (*Blood Wedding,* 1939, and *The House of Bernarda Alba,* written 1936, produced 1945), and T. S. Eliot (*Murder in the Cathedral,* 1935).

Finally, a list of "plays of ideas" should include some other plays by Shaw (*Major Barbara,* 1905, *Man and Superman,* 1905, *Heartbreak House,* 1920) and Pirandello (*Right You Are, If You Think You Are,* 1917, *Henry IV,* 1922), as well as contemporary philosophical drama (usually existentialist) by Jean-Paul Sartre (*The Flies,* 1943, *No Exit,* 1944) and Albert Camus

(*Caligula*, 1944), and what might be called the anti-philosophical plays of Samuel Beckett (*Waiting for Godot*, 1953, *Endgame*, 1957).

Further examples of contemporary drama from the various categories are mentioned in Chapter Seven.

Part Two

Concepts of
Reality
in the Great Periods of Drama

PRE-ELIZABETHAN DRAMA

Conventions of Ancient Greek Drama

Since the dramatists of the twentieth century conceive of reality in several different ways and present it through a variety of techniques, playwright and play-reader are faced with a kind of mutual responsibility. On the one hand, the writer must, directly or indirectly, make his frame of reference clear to the reader. But, even more important, the reader must make a conscious effort to understand the level of reality on which a play is operating before the full potential of the dramatic experience can be realized. And if this is true of the plays of our own day, it is even more true when we approach the great plays of the past.

The source of most of the difficulty presented by older plays is not that the playwrights of earlier ages wrote about kinds of reality that are basically different from those that concern modern dramatists and theatergoers. Shakespeare and Sophocles, fully as much as Strindberg or Shaw or O'Neill, were concerned with the level of reality at which the individual confronts the ultimate and inescapable forces, within or outside himself, that control his destiny. And the earlier dramatists, as much as the modern, tried to represent the human condition in terms that their own age would accept as universal. What seems foreign to us, then, is the

78   dramatic language—not the reality itself so much as the conventions by which it is represented.

The conventions of the theater, in common with most of the forms and proprieties of man's social life, have changed steadily through the years. We may feel slightly awkward and at a loss in the presence of the stage practices of Restoration England or ancient Greece, just as we might feel clumsy and uncouth in the court of Charles the Second. We are creatures of the twentieth century, and it takes a little conscious effort, as well as experience, to acclimate ourselves to the usages of another era. But if we can adjust to the expressionism of O'Neill or to the fantasy of Wilder, very little more is demanded of us by the plays of Marlowe or of Aeschylus. As a matter of fact, the distance between realistic and nonrealistic drama in our own day is greater in many ways than that between the conventions of the modern nonrealistic stage and those of Elizabethan or Greek drama. And in reading the latter, as in reading Strindberg or O'Neill or Wilder, we need to make some effort to identify the conventions that are operating, to know what they were designed to do, and to accept them in the spirit in which they were intended.

Since the civilization that flourished during the fifth century B.C. in Greece or, more specifically, in Athens, was both literally and figuratively far removed from our own, it is not surprising that its theatrical conventions should differ from ours in almost every respect. In order to read Greek tragedy intelligently, it is not absolutely necessary to understand every aspect of its theory and practice. Matters of physical staging, for instance, are fascinating and often illuminating, but they are of more value to the scholar than to the amateur. For the average reader most of the difficulties are presented by a fairly specific group of conventions; and once these are understood and accepted, Greek drama becomes much more intelligible. In the order of their increasing relevance to the kind of reality being represented, these conventions are: the formality and "artificiality" of the language; the nondramatic, lyrical passages; the use of the chorus; the rigidly restricted number of actors that could be used; and the treatment

Concepts of Reality in the Great Periods of Drama

of the Olympian gods. In considering these conventions in greater detail, we need to remember that the three major Greek playwrights, Aeschylus, Sophocles, and Euripides, did not always use them in exactly the same way, and the differences will also throw light on the significant changes in Greek tragedy over its hundred-year development.

When we come to Greek drama for the first time, the element that immediately strikes us as unfamiliar is the apparent stiffness of the language. A translator will sometimes try to circumvent this obstacle by the heavy use of colloquialisms and even slang. But contemporary "everyday" language does nothing to help recreate the authentic atmosphere or impact of a Greek play. Formality and dignity of speech can be as organic a part of drama as *what* is said. Were Shakespeare's plays modernized—as, fortunately, they are not, except in spelling and punctuation—and reduced to twentieth-century colloquial idiom, the slight gain in a more intelligible vocabulary would scarcely compensate for the loss of nearly every other quality of form or feeling that makes his plays what they are. And the same point might be made about the highly specialized and poetic language of modern playwrights such as Synge or T. S. Eliot. So, too, the language of Aeschylus and Sophocles is not Greek slang. Therefore, whereas a good translation of a Greek play need not be excessively archaic or stiff, it should, even when rendered in prose rather than poetry, retain the grace, the rhythms, the poetic and formal language that it would have had for its original audience, and that are consistent with the formality, the distance from everyday reality, of all the other elements in the play.

A more specific source of difficulty, or at least of a sense of strangeness, is the strong lyrical element in Greek drama. Of course, if we are accustomed to Shakespeare's blank verse, the poetic form of the dialogue and the sometimes lengthy monologues will not seem strange; but not even Shakespeare will prepare us for the lyrical poetry of the Greek choral odes. These odes, which appear at fairly regular intervals, were literally songs, and as such they were normally distinct from what we would call

Pre-Elizabethan Drama

the "action" of a play. It would be a mistake, however, to look on these lyrical passages either as intruding or as undramatic. It seems likely that in its earliest and unrecorded stages Greek drama consisted almost entirely of choral odes, perhaps punctuated by brief episodes illustrating the events being commemorated, but even then probably consisting of little more than a dialogue between the leader of the chorus and one other figure. In the course of time, the emphasis shifted from the lyrical and narrative to the dramatic, and the odes remained largely as a device by which the playwright could make some further comment, at least indirectly, on the characters or action or theme of his play.

Probably the best analogy to the choral ode in modern drama might be the break between the acts of a play; and in fact the Greek custom is the source of the five-act structure of Roman drama, which in turn is parent, by way of the late Elizabethans, to our own common three-act division. But, while the ode may have interrupted the action, it was not an intermission for chatter or for whatever the Greek equivalent of smoking may have been. For one thing, there was something going on well worth paying attention to. The odes were not only sung by the chorus, but danced, making a combination of opera and ballet the exact form of which we can only imagine. As in the case of the modern intermission, this musical interlude provided a temporary relaxation of dramatic tension and sometimes suggested the passage of a certain amount of time, though usually not more than a few hours. Even so, the pause in the flow of the action should not be viewed as a break so much as a bridge and a bond that was part of the thematic and structural development of the play.

The choric ode was used for a variety of purposes. It might present the thinly veiled utterances of the playwright, or it might speak only for the specific group, usually of "townspeople," that it was supposed to represent. But in almost every case it pushes our thinking or our feeling in a specific direction and so adds an important dimension to the play. The great advantage of this convention is that, while the chorus is usually part of the more or less "realistic" action of a play, during the ode it momentarily moves outside the action so that it can express its ideas directly to the audience, rather after the fashion of a group soliloquy. In unburdening its soul, so to speak, the chorus may express significant doubts about the wisdom or probity of one of the characters; it may draw some moral lesson from the action recently staged; it may suggest analogies, in other stories or myths, to the problems and dilemmas of a major character and thus broaden the implications of the play; it may, by stating its own thoughts, heighten the mood of despair or fear or anticipation for the audience; or it may, by expressing a hope or a judgment that we would like to share but that is disappointed completely in the subsequent action, contribute effectively to dramatic irony.

A choral ode implies a chorus, and the presence of the group itself, rather than its songs, may disturb the modern reader. The chorus, although its singing and dancing are limited to the odes, is usually present as part of the dramatis personae through much of the play.[1] The operettas and musical comedies of our own day provide a partial analogy to the Greek chorus. In the works of Gilbert and Sullivan, for example, there is always a chorus of sailors, young maidens, or the like, either on stage or on the verge of trooping in, ready to burst into song at any excuse, or none; and we do not balk at so delightful a convention. The difference is, of course, that the modern musical comedy chorus need be justified only on aesthetic grounds, whereas the ancient chorus must be rationalized in dramatic terms; and the periodic presence of a group of from twelve to fifteen persons with relatively little to do except during the choral odes seems to us both unrealistic and cumbersome. Since most conventions represent in some sense a "short cut to reality," we may well wonder exactly what kind of reality made the chorus the necessary and durable tradition that it was.

It is sometimes said that the chorus in a Greek tragedy represents in its make-up and responses the average or "ideal" observer

---

[1] It may help the modern reader to remember that the chorus spoke *as a group* only in the choral odes. In the dialogue of the play, it was normally only the *leader* of the chorus who spoke.

—that it is the agent, as it were, of the audience itself. As a generalization this is helpful, but it needs considerable qualification in specific instances. If, as seems likely, Greek drama developed out of religious ritual, some kind of identification between audience and chorus would be most natural. These early religious ceremonies, as was suggested in Chapter One, were probably civic affairs, in which the community as a whole acknowledged the power of, and attempted to placate, the mysterious and imponderable forces that so directly governed its life. When what may at first have been simply a choric chant of praise or supplication became quasi-dramatic, the leader of the chorus and perhaps one other person took on the roles of figures in some significant incident in their religious myth, which was then acted out. But the chorus as a whole remained as a "cloud of witnesses," as worshipers—in other words, as representatives of the community, standing for its members or with them in the presence of some elemental mystery.

The nature of the mystery changed as man became less directly concerned with the brute facts of his physical environment and had time to contemplate the enigma of his moral and social nature. As long as Greek tragedy was in a real sense communal in nature, however, the chorus remained an organic element in the drama. And if the members of the audience identified themselves with it, this was not because what the chorus said or did was "ideal" or what *they* would have done (indeed, the obtuseness and helplessness of the chorus is often very irritating), but because, as a group, it represented the idea of a community as such.

In particular cases, the way in which the chorus reflects the point of view of the community may not be immediately obvious. The chorus of Sea Nymphs in Aeschylus' *Prometheus Bound* is not literally human—but then, neither is the play. On the other hand, the nymphs do remind us constantly of Prometheus' service to the human community and present us with a consistently human angle of vision, in sharp contrast to the inhuman and inflexible tyranny of Zeus. So, too, the Furies in the *Eumenides*, the last play of the Oresteian trilogy, are nonhuman figures. And if they represent human impulses, they are those of eye-for-eye and blood-for-blood revenge, which may lie deep in the instinctive nature of the individuals who make up society, but which are hardly social. However, the play is in part *about* the triumph of a more civilized concept of justice over the primitive and instinctive code that once governed the community. At the end of the play, the Furies agree to compromise their code of blood by accepting the supremacy of law and order in the form of the jury —that is, the modern community. The more common practice, however, as exemplified in the same poet's *Agamemnon* and *Seven Against Thebes,* was to let the chorus embody the communal point of view specifically by making its members citizens of the communities involved. As elders of Argos or of Thebes in these two plays, the choral members are directly concerned with the welfare of the community as a whole; but they are equally sensitive to the fortunes of their rulers and leaders. The community is intimately involved in the fall of its king, for his tragedy is not that of a single man but of mankind.

Another convention of the Greek theater, and one that to modern eyes seems far more mechanical and arbitrary, is the limited number of actors that could take part in a play. We need not go into the tradition that Aeschylus introduced the second actor (in addition to the single actor plus chorus that had been the custom previously), or that Sophocles added the third and Euripides, even more. The number of actors, since each might play several roles, does not in itself affect our understanding of the plays. The convention deserves notice, however, because the increase in the number of actors available to play different roles in the works of the three playwrights parallels a shift in the function of the chorus and a change in the kind of tragedy that was written.

Insofar as it is safe to generalize about Aeschylus, most of his plays seem to focus on a single tragic situation. In them we do not usually witness a series of *events* leading gradually and fatefully to a tragic denouement. We are not shown the slow steps by which the complexities of human personality coalesce with the

Pre-Elizabethan Drama

twists of fate to produce catastrophe. The dramatic development does not reveal *how* a situation came about; rather, it explores the moral, the human, the emotional implications of a given situation.

The *Agamemnon* is above all a play of waiting. We know (or the Greek audience did) that Clytemnestra will kill her husband; she knows it, having made up her mind before the play opens; and Cassandra makes the impending disaster explicit to the fearful chorus. The dominant atmosphere of the play is one of frightened anticipation; and nothing that *happens* either hinders or contributes to the disaster all await. The movement of the play, then, is not in the action but in the slow intensification of our feelings about an established situation.

In *Prometheus Bound* the only constants are Prometheus and the chorus (and perhaps the imaginatively created image of Zeus in the background). The drama exists largely in the series of dialogues between the crucified Titan and his various visitors, each of which illuminates further Prometheus' nature and the clash between his inflexible will and the equally unyielding power of Zeus.

The *Eumenides* is a very different sort of play, and at least on the surface it contains more of what we regard as action. Still, the drama lies not in what happens to Orestes but in the confrontation of two moral codes—that of Apollo, put into practice by Orestes; and that of the Furies, that matricide, however provoked, is a violation of the moral law and must be punished. The drama reaches its climax in the trial scene, in which the Furies with their passionate claims of vengeance are brought face to face with Apollo, and the conflict is made explicit and entirely verbal. The *Eumenides* is undoubtedly a "play of ideas"; and Aeschylus recognized, two thousand years before George Bernard Shaw, the drama inherent in a clash between opposed points of view or moral positions. And, like Shaw, Aeschylus presents the conflict through "talk, talk, talk." The characters are not complicated and rounded individuals so much as representatives of a particular viewpoint, or a particular kind of moral blindness. The reality here is not the complex contradictions and paradoxes of human nature but the actuality and unavoidableness of moral law. In this kind of drama the chorus, whether it takes a specific stand or simply underlines the conflicting positions of other characters, plays a significant part in clarifying the issues and implications of the situation being explored. And there is no need for a large number of actors.

It would be misleading to suggest that Sophocles' use of the chorus or the number of actors differed basically from that of Aeschylus. There is, however, a shift in emphasis in his plays that is reflected in a slightly different use of these conventions. On the whole, Sophocles was more interested than Aeschylus in the complexities and ambiguities of human nature. Aeschylus' heroes— Prometheus, Eteocles, Agamemnon, Orestes—are rather one-sided figures, driven by a single belief or passion or obsession. We cannot say of them, as we can of Sophocles' protagonists, that there but for a single weakness goes a truly good or noble man. Aristotle's comments on the tragic flaw, the one unfortunate quality that leads to the downfall of a man otherwise better or nobler than the ordinary, do apply to most of Sophocles' plays.[2] The focus, in other words, is on the individual personality, with its curious mixture of elements, its conflicting impulses, its incongruous juxtaposition of good and bad, and on the ways in which these diverse qualities, confronted by the inexorable realities of the world around him, can lead a man to his destruction.

Sophocles best brings out this many-sidedness of human nature by presenting his central figure in a variety of situations and in interaction with a variety of personalities. We see Oedipus at his noblest and most virtuous as he promises to track down the source of the plague in Thebes at whatever cost to himself; in his angry rebuff of Tiresias' warning we see his pride; we see more of his rash anger in the story of his killing the stranger at the crossroads; we glimpse something of the depths of his humanity

[2]Aristotle describes the tragic hero as a man who is "above the common level," but who "is not eminently good and just, yet whose misfortune is brought about not by vice or depravity, but by some error or frailty." *On the Art of Poetry,* ed. Nahm, pp. 16 and 20 (secs. XIII and XV).

in the joy and relief he feels at the news from Corinth, followed by the growing, numbing horror as the answers to the questions he cannot help but ask lead in one terrible direction; and we see the awesome image of guilt linked with moral dignity in his self-punishment. The fusion of contradictory elements that make up the personality of Creon, in Sophocles' *Antigone,* is revealed through a series of dramatic episodes. In his initial dialogue with the chorus, Creon is sincerely dedicated to his responsibilities as king, placing the good of the state above that of any individual, even the ruler. This, surely, is an admirable man, and fortunate is the state ruled by a king with such respect for the laws. Yet Creon is harsh and inflexible in his interpretation of those laws when he denounces Antigone; he is proud and cannot listen to the sound advice of his son; he is quick-tempered and arrogant in his taunting reply to Tiresias' warning; and, after the admonitions of the chorus send him hurrying to undo what can never be undone and he is faced with his responsibility for the suicides of his wife and son, this once-noble character falls to pieces before our eyes.

Paradoxically, as the focus of tragedy shifts to the inner conflicts and dilemmas born of the meeting between man's divided nature and the contradictory demands and obligations of civilized life, the need increases for overt action to make that conflict dramatic. The drama and the tragedy lie not in a situation, which can be talked about, but in a process, an interaction of cause and effect, which must "happen" and the implications of which must be recognized, gradually, by the protagonist and by us. Creon is tragic not, as Agamemnon was, because of his blind, unyielding self-centeredness but because he is a conscientious man, sincerely if somewhat pigheadedly trying to do the right thing, who because of his single blind spot sets in motion an inexorable series of events that in turn rebounds on him and destroys him. So it is that Sophocles' plays have more complex action and more fully developed plots than do those of Aeschylus. The episodes are no longer a series of comments on a single situation but parts of a tightly linked chain of events that leads directly to a tragic denouement. Further, the chorus is in general less a source of commentary and more an actor, taking part in the action and entering into conversations that serve to draw out and dramatize the personalities of the major characters. This greater complexity, it should be noted, is not a sign that Sophocles is a better playwright than Aeschylus; he simply writes about a different aspect of human experience.

In placing greater emphasis on plot, Sophocles makes more use also of what might be called "story appeal," an audience's quite natural interest in what happens next. Although our attention in *Oedipus* is centered on the king's slow realization of his true situation, the element of suspense is very strong indeed. And far from destroying this effect, our presumed foreknowledge of the outcome of the story only increases our interest in Oedipus' response to each new situation and revelation as it arises. In *Antigone,* too, we become caught up in the question of what possible resolution there can be for the conflicting loyalties of Creon and Antigone. In a less well known but equally fine play, *Philoctetes,* the dramatic drive comes largely from the question of how Neoptolemus will solve the dilemma of conflicting loyalties: Will he follow his natural human sympathies for the plight of Philoctetes, or will he honor his promises to Odysseus and the Greeks and betray his friend? Because Neoptolemus makes the "right" decision and a literal *deus ex machina* appears to confirm it and to reassure him that he will not suffer for his choice, the play is removed from the category of tragedy and becomes a kind of moral melodrama.

A strong plot-line with its consequent tendency toward melodrama was developed even further by Euripides; many of his plays might properly be called tragicomedies, in which the interest lies in the excitement of the action rather than in any serious comment on life. But even the plays that are, properly speaking, tragedies emphasize not the complexities of character, nor its development and drawing self-awareness, but what happens *because* of man's nature. Most of Euripides' characters, rather like those of Aeschylus, are men or women caught up in some overwhelming passion or plunged in the darkness of some abysmal

moral blindness. They are more violent, though, and what fasci-
nates Euripides is not that in the narrowness of their vision they
violate the moral order and must suffer for it but that they are
tightly in the grip of forces over which they seem to have no
control and which destroy both them and those around them.
Medea, for example, is no Sophoclean heroine, a good woman
with a fatal weakness. The term "tragic flaw" seems almost trivial
when applied to such a whirlwind of passion and vengeance.
Phaedra's passion for Hippolytus is not a single blemish in an
otherwise noble queen; it is a blazing fire that no amount of
reason and self-control can subdue and that consumes not only
her but the object of her love and, in a sense, her husband
Theseus as well.

Unlike Sophocles, Euripides does not trace the moral and psychological implications of man's divided nature, nor does he see
the individual alone as suffering for his inability to find a way out
of his dilemma. It is true that all Thebes is involved in Oedipus'
guilt and discovery, and that Creon's stubbornness leads directly
to the deaths of his son and wife; but Sophocles portrays the
suffering of others as part of the "punishment" of the tragic hero,
part of the price *he* must pay for his blindness. It seems wholly
inadequate, on the other hand, to think of Medea's murder of
her children as in any sense a punishment for her hate and revenge
—it is part *of* it; nor is Phaedra in any way punished in the suffering of Hippolytus and Theseus. Sophocles, for all the grand scope
of his plays, tends to sum up in one individual both the paradox
and the tragedy of human experience; Euripides paints a larger
and more gaudy canvas. He looks at man as a social animal: No
man is free, and all are involved in a common guilt. A Medea or
a Phaedra blazes into the world destroying indiscriminately the
wicked and the innocent, not because of some hidden flaw but as
a consequence of her humanity. Medea's tragedy is that she is
what she is, and ours is that she exists.

In dramatizing the overwhelming and uncontrollable forces
that govern human nature and the consequences they bring,
Euripides almost inevitably turns to violent and melodramatic

Concepts of Reality in the Great Periods of Drama

plots. In some of his plays the strong plot-line breaks down, and we are presented with several melodramatic episodes that illustrate or focus on a single theme. But, in either case, the kind of tragedy that Euripides wrote demanded a further increase in the number of actors in a given play and simultaneously reduced the usefulness of the chorus, which, in a few of the plays, such as the *Medea,* becomes a distinct nuisance. It is largely for these reasons—the more numerous dramatis personae and the demotion of the chorus to a largely decorative function—as well as for the pessimism of his outlook, that Euripides has earned the dubious honor of being called the most modern of the ancients.

Euripides has been termed "modern" also because in many of his plays he appears to take a skeptical if not downright disrespectful view of the Olympian gods; and since in the twentieth century it is a little hard to take the Greek gods seriously, we think we see in this playwright a kindred spirit. At this distance, it is difficult to tell exactly how seriously any of the Greek playwrights took the traditional deities. Euripides sometimes makes a god look very silly indeed, although elsewhere the deities exert a genuine and powerful force on the action of a play. On the other hand, the relatively conventional appearance of the gods in the plays of Aeschylus and Sophocles does not necessarily mean that they "believed" in those anthropomorphic figures in any literal sense. But since the gods do have a significant function in most Greek tragedies, it would seem more relevant to treat the deities simply as a convention and to investigate the uses of that convention than to guess at the relative religiosity of the playwrights.

Hardest for a modern reader to accept in the Greek gods is their amorality and their capriciousness. Most of us think of a deity as good and just and in some way the foundation of a consistent and coherent natural and moral law. The Olympian deities, however, seem arbitrary, unjust, jealous of their powers and of each other and, aside from certain favorites among the mortals, completely unconcerned with the welfare of mankind. If, however, we remember that belief in these gods probably grew out of primitive efforts to explain uncontrollable and inexplicable phenomena in both the physical world and human nature, their behavior seems more intelligible and more consistent.

It will help, then, to look at the gods essentially as symbols, representing those elements in the external world or in human nature that are beyond the control of the individual and from which there is no appeal. In these general terms, all three Greek writers of tragedy use the gods in similar ways; but there are individual differences in emphasis. When Aeschylus brings the gods into his plays, they appear to stand for a code or moral law that mortals may violate only at their peril but that is neither eternal nor necessarily "right." In *Prometheus Bound,* Zeus is the embodiment of an arbitrary and inflexible law that Prometheus, by committing an act that is good in human terms, has violated. For this Prometheus must suffer; but it is hinted that at some future time Zeus will take on the attribute of mercy in addition to his stern justice, and Prometheus will be freed. Before the Oresteian trilogy opens, Agamemnon, more concerned, in his pride and selfishness, with his success as leader of the Greeks than with family bonds, sacrifices his daughter Iphigenia to the gods to win favorable winds for Troy. The law of blood demands Agamemnon's life, and it is his wife, Clytemnestra, who in the first play of the trilogy exacts the penalty. Her own motives are hardly pure, however, for by her act she frees herself to marry her lover, Aegisthus. In the *Choephori,* Orestes continues this chain reaction of retributive justice by murdering his mother. Although his motives *are* pure, or at least unselfish, and his revenge on Clytemnestra has Apollo's sanction, Orestes too has committed a serious crime against the family and therefore against society, and the Furies demand that he suffer as well. The implication is that the law of retributive justice, of blood for blood, approved though it may be by Apollo, can lead to nothing better than an endless chain of revenge, and revenge for revenge. At the end of the *Eumenides* another deity, Athena, steps in and replaces the primitive code of murder and retribution with a law of order and justice, by which guilt and punishment are not determined either by the individual or by the gods, but by society

Concepts of Reality in the Great Periods of Drama

represented in a jury. The old order changes, but, before it does, the old law has exacted a terrible price in blood and suffering.

In Sophocles' plays the gods rarely appear in their own persons but are constantly in the background, either through their oracles or in repeated allusions. Here they seem to be less the embodiments of moral forces than symbols of *all* those elements in life which inevitably limit and impinge on man's existence, whether we call them laws or natural forces or simply Fate. A characteristic pattern involves a character who defies or tries to escape the oracle of the gods, only to discover that there are powers in the universe beyond man's will or comprehension. It is sometimes said of Sophocles that his plays demonstrate the helplessness of the individual before a predetermined Fate. This is a gross distortion; and Sophocles is not "demonstrating" anything. There is no drama in absolute determinism. Fate, or the gods, standing for all the irrational and inexorable forces outside man's ken, are certainly present; but the drama Sophocles is contemplating is that of the way in which noble, imperfect, blind man accepts or does not accept—defies and is destroyed by—this absolute reality. Oedipus and his parents before him have done everything possible to prove the fateful oracle false, and yet every wriggle they make only brings them closer to fulfilling its prediction. Sophocles is interested not primarily in the *fact* of the fatality but in the way in which a single representative human faces his fate.

Paradoxically, it is in the plays of Euripides, so often regarded as a skeptic, that the Olympian gods are most in evidence. As in Sophocles, they seem to represent inexorable forces that man cannot control, but here they are associated more with elements in human nature itself—inherent in man, and in that sense natural and real, but at the same time uncontrollable and destructive. The gods could be called the irrational in man.

The hate of Medea, the passion of Phaedra and the purity of Hippolytus (symbolized respectively by their exclusive worship of Aphrodite and Artemis), the religious frenzy of the worshipers of Dionysus, are not in themselves abnormal constituents of man's nature. They may ordinarily be balanced and controlled by other

Pre-Elizabethan Drama

qualities, even by equally irrational ones; but they are part of our nature, and they defy reason. Phaedra does not will to love Hippolytus, nor does Medea will herself into a hatred so profound that it consumes her children; they are both in the grip of a power beyond their will. In this sense, then, for Euripides the gods are *within* man but not controlled by him. They are a little like the Original Sin of Christianity: Without them man would not be man, but with them he destroys himself and those around him. They are the origin of the anguish of man's existence—but also, one might add, of its joy and splendor.

In one way or another the gods are basic to the tragic vision of all the Greek playwrights. They represent, in differing ways, the implacable and impersonal forces in the world's and in man's nature, beyond the reach of his reason and his will, that are a part of his existence and a source of his tragedy. Essentially, then, the gods stand for the mystery of human experience, and for that reason they are very much a part of the reality of Greek drama. With its gods and its communal chorus and poetic language, Greek tragedy constantly directs our attention away from particular situations and people toward universal forces and qualities. The irrational, the imponderable, the unknowable—these have always haunted man's imagination and shaken his security. And he is great, and tragic, not when he pretends he knows all the answers or ignores the questions but when he does what he must do in spite of danger and fear. Thus tragedy lies in the confrontation, or conjunction, of the reality of human consciousness and will with the reality of all the mysterious internal and external forces that limit and frustrate that will.

Death and Rebirth: Roman Drama; Medieval Liturgical Plays; Miracle and Morality Plays

Although drama of the stature of Greek tragedy did not appear again in Europe until the latter part of the sixteenth century, dramatic activity seems never to have ceased altogether. Of course, Rome, at its height, caught for a brief moment the reflected splendor of Greek drama. The comedies of Plautus (*ca.* 254–184 B.C.) show considerable literary polish, but they are little more than clever adaptations of late Greek comedy. Terence (190–159 B.C.) appears to have been more original in his rewriting; but even though his plays are constructed with a great deal of technical skill, they are farcical and superficial. The plays of Seneca (4 B.C.–A.D. 65), written for the study and weighted down with moral aphorisms, are mere academic exercises compared to the Greek tragedies they imitate. Roman drama in general is conspicuously part of a dying tradition; it is important not in itself but for its influence on later French and English drama.

During the final years of the Roman Empire, the debauched and overripe remnant of the art form that had been one of the glories of Classical civilization was destroyed by the growing power of the Christian Church. Nothing of great value was lost, unless possibly the historical continuity of a tradition—and at that point in history the tradition had ceased to have any value. The darkness of the so-called Dark Ages has been widely disputed by historians; but there is no question that the theaters of the Western world were quite dark enough. From roughly the fifth century to the tenth, records of anything that could legitimately be called dramatic activity are lacking. During this period there seem to have been wandering minstrels, acrobats, and mimes, traveling singly or in groups, who may have performed crude improvisations along the lines of a vaudeville skit. It seems likely that a certain amount of spontaneous "folk drama" existed. But of all this nothing is certain. It is apparent, however, that in some way or another the craft of acting was kept alive, in whatever debased form, until the climate became more favorable to the rebirth of the theater.

One of history's many ironies is the fact that the Church, which in the late Roman period had been instrumental in suppressing the theater as an enemy of religion, provided the soil in which its new growth took place. The liturgical plays, as church-sponsored dramas are called, differed greatly in content and purpose from the licentious theater of Rome. They were based on Biblical figures and events, and their aim was didactic—to teach a lesson. Yet, like all drama, they were based on the ideas that the mimetic representation of an action is pleasurable and that a story is more effective when it is *dramatic*. And the purpose of these plays was to bring home to the uneducated the facts and faith of Christianity.

To the modern reader, the early Miracle Plays (known also as Mystery Plays), which evolved in England in the twelfth or thirteenth century and were popular well into the reign of Queen Elizabeth, seem crude in the extreme. And indeed they are, although in their simplicity many of them possess a kind of elemental power that more sophisticated plays lack. They are discussed here, however, less because of their dramatic merit than because of the light they throw on later, and especially Elizabethan, drama. They are among the principal formative influences on the great flowering of drama that marked the final decade of the sixteenth century. And, because of their relative simplicity, we can see in them significant features that become obscured, even though they remain just as important, in the works of such men as Marlowe, Shakespeare, and John Webster.

Although the Miracle Plays were in every sense religious, being based on Biblical subjects and sponsored at least originally by the Church, the most striking thing about them is not their piety or high seriousness so much as their easy informality. They possess a sense of familiarity and even intimacy with figures and events of the past that is achieved largely by a cheerful disregard for the facts and changes of history.

One of the best known and certainly the most delightful of the Miracle Plays is the so-called *Second Shepherds' Play*. Part of a cycle that has become known as the Towneley Plays, it was written by an unknown author during the late fourteenth or early fifteenth century and was produced in the town of Wakefield, England. The title derives not from the number of shepherds involved but from the fact that this is the second play in the cycle to deal with the appearance of the angel, announcing the birth of

Christ, to the shepherds outside Bethlehem and their subsequent adoration of the infant Jesus in the manger. There is much human appeal in this tale of simple rustics, dumbfounded by their glimpse of heavenly glory and presenting their humble gifts to the Son of God. It is still frequently re-enacted as a Christmas pageant, and to the farmers and herdsmen of rural England it would have been the most meaningful of all the episodes associated with the Nativity. The author of *The Second Shepherds' Play* strengthens the feeling of immediacy by building on the brief Biblical passage an involved and vastly amusing farce about Mak, the sheepstealer, who tries unsuccessfully to pass off a stolen lamb as his wife's newborn child. Only when the shepherds have turned the laugh on Mak and tossed him in a blanket does the angel appear, and the group troops off to Bethlehem.

What is most interesting about this version of the story, however, is that the characters and setting are by no stretch of the imagination those of Palestine in the first century; they are those of northern England in the fifteenth. The characters bear such homely English names as Mak, Coll, Gib, and Daw. Their talk is of local problems—the harshness of the winter that year, their oppression by the landlords, their grievances against the government, the hardship of having a nagging wife and many children. The countryside, both in description and in place names, is that around Wakefield. And the story itself is just such a rough tale as might have been told around a campfire after a hard day on the Yorkshire moors.

The Second Shepherds' Play is not entirely representative of the Miracle Plays. Its plot and characterization are more skillfully developed than most, and the secular element is more obvious. Even so, the play is typical of the tendency of these relatively primitive playwrights to translate Biblical stories into contemporary terms. We must avoid the temptation, however, to attribute this tendency to simple-mindedness or ignorance on the part of either writers or audiences. Certainly, one of the motives behind this practice was to bring the Bible stories home to an illiterate audience, to make them feel that the coming of Christ was of personal significance to *them*. But the important point is that the value of historical accuracy for its own sake would probably never have entered their heads. For playwrights and audience alike, the changes wrought by time between Judea under the Caesars and England under Henry V were accidents of history and were not significant. If someone had asked a spectator at *The Second Shepherds' Play* if that were the way it had really happened, he would have been surprised that anyone should question it. If pressed, he might have admitted that the names of people and places would be different and foreign-sounding, that the characters would have worn different clothes and suffered under different rulers; but in all important respects the story would be "true."

This tendency to blur historical distinctions and to create the illusion that Biblical events took place amidst people who differed in no essential respect from the audience, also accounts in part for the mixture of comic and serious elements that is characteristic of the Miracle Play. In classical drama, tragedy and comedy were kept rigidly separate; but life itself does not fall neatly into such black-and-white categories, and part of the realism of the Miracle Play lies in its juxtaposition of the solemn and the ridiculous. And while the intrusion of comedy into religious plays probably came as a result of the perfectly normal human desire for fun—they were performed as part of holiday celebrations—it had a definite moral function. Laughter often represents an expression of contempt, arising from our awareness of the incongruity, ridiculousness, or folly of its object. In the Miracle Play, it was characteristically the figures who were spiritually blind or out of balance that became the subjects of comedy. The first comic roles appear to have been those of what we would call the villains of the Bible—Cain, Herod, Pontius Pilate, even the devils themselves. But more humble persons also were the objects of laughter, men and women whose single-minded pursuit of pleasure or gain made them seem incongruous and comical when set against the characters who had harkened to the Divine Will. Such are the gossipy friends of Noah's wife, and even Mrs. Noah herself, all much too busy tippling on ale to heed the warnings of her husband; and such is the farcical sheep thief Mak, whose ridiculous "newborn child," a lamb stolen to fill his stomach, is set in comic juxtaposition with the infant Lamb of God. The qualities that make these figures the object of laughter are the qualities that made them familiar and plausible to the fifteenth-century audience—in other words, qualities that are universal and timeless.

The element of universality in medieval drama was further enhanced by the absence of any kind of particularized stage setting. The Roman theater had used a highly conventionalized set, representing a house front or a street leading from the harbor to the forum, which remained unchanged throughout a play. Simple as it was, however, this set gave a visual identity and limit to the time and place of the action. The Miracle Play, on the other hand, whether produced on a fixed scaffold or on a pageant wagon, was innocent of any setting that would identify the geographical or historical placing of the action. Where the playing space was large enough, specific areas of it might be allotted to particular uses—one end might contain the Throne of God and the other Hellmouth—but the mortal world in between was between time and space and was specified only by the identity and speech of the character holding the stage. This universal stage, which could be whatever and set whenever it was said to be, added tremendously to the audience's sense that what it was witnessing was not an historical event but a timeless truth.

The parallels that the spectator would have seen in the Miracle Play were not simply between Biblical events and his contemporary world but between the various episodes themselves, for the habit of thinking by analogy was very much a part of the medieval mind. The fall of Satan was repeated in the fall of Adam and had a parallel in the later fall of Judas. The pride of Pharaoh was also the pride of Herod and Pilate. Abraham's willing sacrifice of his son had its analogue in God's sacrifice of His Son for the sake of Man. Since these little plays depicting the major stories of the Bible were brought together as a "cycle," stretching from the Creation to the Day of Judgment, and were played consecutively on a single day, the parallels would have been apparent and significant. The cycle plays really were a representation of two things, the nature of man and the will of God; and these were seen as absolutes beyond history and change. But if the cycle, in its "plot," constituted a kind of divine history of the world, it was also by analogy a history of the individual, from his birth in sin, through his struggle with the temptations of this world, to his death and judgment. And the figures in this drama, although given Biblical names, could for the most part be viewed as embodying the various human and divine qualities that are the determining forces in man's spiritual journey through life. It would not be difficult, then, for an audience's imagination to move from a play about characters called Herod or Judas to one about figures called Pride or Covetousness.

There is, in fact, a late Miracle Play (late 15th century) dealing with Mary Magdalene that, in addition to such "historical" figures as Herod, Pilate, and Caesar, has characters called Flesh, Pride, Sloth, and Lechery. The device is carried much further in the Morality Play, a generic name for plays in which all the dramatis personae are given labels representing some moral abstraction, such as Envy, Lust, Penance, or Mercy. This type of drama did not grow out of the Miracle tradition but existed alongside it in the late Middle Ages, and the *Mary Magdalene* mentioned above was not so much a transition between two popular forms as a hybrid of them.

Characteristically, the Morality Play deals with the life of a generalized figure called Mankind or Everyman, from his birth, through a life in which he vacillates between the temptations of the World, the Flesh, and the Devil and the admonitions of Wisdom, Righteousness, or Penance, to his repentance, death, and salvation. Sometimes the play ends with a debate between Mercy and Justice regarding the disposition of man's soul, with Mercy having the last word. Probably the best-known play of this type is the relatively late *Everyman,* performed in the early sixteenth century. Here the story is less panoramic and begins only when

Death warns Everyman to prepare for his imminent summons. The heart of the play lies in Everyman's painful discovery that his worldly friends, Good Fellowship, Kindred, Cousin, and Goods, will not "go with him in his most need," and even Beauty, Strength, and Discretion desert him on the road to the grave. Knowledge, who has introduced him to Confession, guides him on his way, but only Good Deeds will stay by him beyond death to the Judgment Seat.

The differences between the Miracle Play and the Morality are so considerable that we might suppose the kind of reality dealt with is different as well. The characters and the action in the latter, rather than being Biblical and therefore in some sense historical, are purely allegorical; and, far from representing human beings in believable human situations, they offer a kind of paradigm of the relationships between virtues and vices that determine man's spiritual health. Whereas the Miracle Play is a divine history of the world, a visual and concrete representation of the subject of man's faith, the Morality Play is concerned primarily with man's behavior in his present life. It is a kind of guidebook to salvation. But the two types differ in method rather than in purpose. In both we still have acted out a typical and universal example, whether in concrete or abstract terms, of man's continuing struggle, with God's help, against the forces of evil. Thus, the reality in both the Miracle Play and the Morality might be defined as man's moral nature.

This tendency of medieval drama, to place man explicitly in the context of a universe governed by moral law, can be contrasted with the view of the human condition taken by Sophocles and Euripides. Although moral values are not wholly irrelevant in their plays, the ultimate reality, the law to which man is bound and which limits his freedom, is essentially amoral—the law of cause and effect, of nature, of human psychology, which man cannot control but must respect. Oedipus and Hippolytus are not morally bad; they have simply run up against inscrutable facts of life that they cannot accept. But in the Miracle and Morality Plays the facts of life are Heaven and Hell, and the conflict and the failure or salvation are usually seen in explicitly moral terms.

SUGGESTIONS FOR READING

Since almost any play is in some sense representative of its time, a supplementary reading list for this essentially historical discussion may perhaps be superfluous. On the other hand, since the approach here has focused as much on the content as on the technique of the plays, substitutions should be made only with careful qualifications and adjustments. It might be helpful to the reader, however, to have in hand a list of plays that can profitably be read in conjunction with those discussed in the text. Again, all are available in inexpensive editions.

Of the Greek playwrights, Aeschylus is probably best represented by the Oresteian trilogy (*Agamemnon, Choephori, The Eumenides*) and *Prometheus Bound;* Sophocles by *Oedipus the King, Antigone, Philoctetes,* and *Oedipus at Colonus;* Euripides by *Electra, Iphigenia in Tauris, Hippolytus, The Bacchae.* An excellent general discussion, which includes analyses of specific plays, is H. D. F. Kitto's *Greek Tragedy* (New York, 1950), a book to which I am myself greatly indebted. Of Roman tragedies, Seneca's *Thyestes* is typical, and sufficient.

Of English medieval drama the Wakefield Shepherds' Play (better known as *The Second Shepherds' Play*) is the most readable and the most anthologized, but it is not really representative. *Noah* (Wakefield Cycle), *The Deluge* (Chester Cycle), *The Sacrifice of Isaac* (Brome MS), and *The Birth of Jesus* (York Cycle) are more typical. *Everyman* is the only easily available example of the Morality Play, and it is also the best.

Beginnings: A Merging of Traditions

Elizabethan drama owes a tremendous debt to Classical Greek and Roman drama, but the debt is largely formal. Until they had learned artistic control—a sense of style and structure—from the Classical models, English dramatists could never achieve the highest level of literary art. And once the lesson of artistic form was soundly learned, the quality of their plays took an immense leap forward. But much as the Elizabethans owed to Rome, the heart of their drama, the view of reality it takes, and the methods by which that reality is represented on the stage develop directly out of the Miracle and Morality Plays.

There are, of course, transitional plays, the works of men who were still feeling their way, imitating the newly discovered "ancients" or experimenting with some wholly untried dramatic method; and most of them are interesting as historical rather than literary documents. But even during this period of confusion and experimentation certain significant patterns stand out; and probably the most important is the increasing tendency toward secularization in drama. In the Miracle Plays the strictly Biblical element became less and less the center of attention, and the allegorical characters of the Morality played their roles side by

101

102   side with historical or quasi-historical figures. Medieval English drama, apart from its use of the Bible, had never been much concerned with historical events as such. England's increasing sense of national identity during the Tudor period, however, stimulated a new and widespread interest in national history, evidenced by the publication and immediate popularity of a variety of *Chronicles,* by Fabyan, Holinshed, Stow, and others. It was almost inevitable that this vast storehouse of exciting and patriotically gratifying subject matter should find its way into dramatic representation, first through the back door of the Morality Play, later by the front door of the chronicle play.

Italian romances and *novelle,* or what we would call "short stories"—tales of illicit love and revenge and murder, provided another mine of secular source material that wooed English playwrights away from didactic drama, even though at first many of these stories were put in a moralistic framework. The English had always had a weakness for melodrama, and even the Biblical cycle plays had never been shy about gratifying the popular taste for violence and bloodshed.

The violence of the early Elizabethan stage, however, was as often as not comic. The custom of expanding the humorous possibilities of roles not protected by their sanctity has already been noted in the early Miracle Plays. The devils, and later the "vices" in the Morality Plays, provided endless opportunities for rough and slapstick humor. Humor and piety are by no means mutually exclusive; but in a good many cases the comic element seems to have been present largely for its own sake, and what began as an appendage was in time often wagging the dog.

Apart from representing the end of this process of secularization in drama, which had been going on for some centuries, the period of transition—roughly, the middle years of the sixteenth century—was notable mainly for variety, fusion, and adaptation. Elements and conventions that were part of the native English dramatic tradition were applied to stories from Italian and Classical sources, and the forms and structure of Classical genres were given substance with typically English characters and plots.

The results are difficult to classify, but in general the dominant modes were comedy, both farcical and romantic, and what might best be called a kind of melodrama, based variously on medieval romances, historical and Classical sources, or Italian tales of intrigue.

The one species of drama that was conspicuously lacking was tragedy. In the earlier religious drama, both Miracle and Morality, there had been no such thing as true tragedy. The purpose of these plays had been to instill hope and faith, to bring home the meaning of God's mercy to man, not to arouse fear or pity. It is true that religious drama characteristically represented man confronting the mystery of human experience with his purely human tools, instinct and reason; but, in failing, he acknowledged his helplessness and need for faith and grace. Evil, where it existed, was normally the subject of ridicule and comedy, not tragedy.

Tragedy did exist, but not as a form of drama. There was an old and honorable tradition of historical verse "tragedies" that dated back at least to the fourteenth-century Italian poet Boccaccio. In his *De Casibus Virorum Illustrium* ("concerning the fall of famous men") Boccaccio narrates, in verse form, the stories of a large number of men who, through their own efforts or good fortune, were elevated to positions of power or wealth or happiness, only to have their hopes disappointed and their exultation end in misery or death. Many of these tales, with some additions, were told by Chaucer's Monk in the *Canterbury Tales,* and in the early fifteenth century John Lydgate wrote *The Fall of Princes,* based on a French expansion of Boccaccio's stories. Lydgate's long and, to modern tastes, very dull poem was popular well into the sixteenth century; and around 1550 an extension was written to include examples of "falls" in more recent British history. Although publication was temporarily held up by the royal censor, the additions were later published separately under the explicitly didactic title *A Mirror for Magistrates.*

Behind most of these "fall of princes" stories lay the notion of the Wheel of Fortune, an allegorical representation of the transience of all mortal achievements that was very popular in medieval literature and iconography. The central idea of this allegory is that men, in the blindness of their desire for worldly things and ambition for greatness and power, bind themselves to the spokes of a gigantic wheel turned by the goddess Fortuna. True to their wishes, they are carried to the height of human felicity; but the wheel is ever-turning—what goes up one side must come down the other—and as certainly as they rise by Fortune, so they are hurled down to destruction. Although the emphasis on the transience and instability of this world as compared to the next is Christian and medieval, the goddess Fortuna might be viewed as a kind of Christian equivalent of the Greek concept of Fate, or the gods—forces that control and limit human affairs, but which are beyond man's influence or understanding and which render his intellect and ambition powerless.

We have, in other words, a fairly well developed notion of tragedy, albeit nondramatic, in print and popular around the middle of the sixteenth century. At about the same time we find the first publications in English translations of Greek and Roman plays, mostly tragedies. Under the circumstances, it was almost inevitable that someone should see the possibility of *English* dramatic tragedy. Actually, the earliest experiments along this line were rather clumsy and slavish imitations of Roman models, written in schools and universities as part of holiday entertainments for the students. But it was only a matter of time before the value of the form and structure of Classical drama was recognized, and it could provide the vitality and violence of non-academic popular drama with a new order and unity.

In roughly the years 1560–1580, then, there was a fortunate conjunction of very diverse elements, and Elizabethan drama in general reveals its debt to all these influences. To Classical tragedy it owed its well-developed structure and sense of unity, its five-act form, and its emphasis on the pathos and dignity of its tragic heroes; and to Seneca in particular it owed its much-used theme of revenge. To the poetic Fall of Princes tradition it owed the characteristic subject matter of its tragedy, the rise, fall, and

death of great men. Its plots, on the other hand, were derived
largely from historical chronicles, both native and Classical, and
from Italian *novelle*. From the Morality tradition came its habit
of representing characters as embodiments of specific virtues and
vices; and to the Biblical Miracle Plays it owed its tendency to
consider man in the context of moral law, normally that of Christianity, as well as its panoramic perspective, representing the
whole or a large part of a man's life, rather than focusing only on
its climactic events after the fashion of Classical tragedy.

It was not, however, simply in matters of technique that
Elizabethan drama represented a fusion of elements found in its
diverse origins. Each of the tributary traditions had its own
characteristic way of conceiving reality, or at least was concerned
primarily with one particular *area* of reality. These different kinds
of reality were not mutually exclusive, to be sure, but the emphasis
tended to be in one direction at the expense of others. In one
sense the ultimate reality was always man; but the frame of
reference in which he was seen was not the same. The reality of
the Miracle Play, for example, might be called the reality of
faith—the reality of a divine order and purpose. Man was seen
as part of a Grand Plan, a figure in a gigantic tapestry that was
varied and violent in its scenes of endless struggle between Good
and Evil, but which was framed by the Creation and the Day of
Judgment and was complete and perfect in the Mind of God.
The Biblical events represented in the plays were but the concrete
and visual manifestation of the spiritual order; and because they
too were in the Mind of God, they were timeless and universal.
Adam fell, Christ was born and was crucified, again and again, in
every age, in every land—indeed, in every heart. The reality of
the Miracle Play, then, lay at the level of spiritual truth and was
understood through analogies.

In the Morality Play, as we have seen, the relationship between
human experience and the dramatic event was not so much that
of analogy as one of abstraction. Of course, meaning and relevance were gained in both types of plays by establishing recognizable parallels with human affairs and human nature. But in

the Morality the emphasis was much more on Man per se, the context was specific moral law rather than the Divine Plan, and the scope was not that of the grand pageant from Creation to the end of the world but the goal of the individual soul, Heaven or Hell. The reality with which the Morality Play was concerned was the particular moral qualities which constituted man's nature, his pride and lust and conscience; and because it dealt so explicitly and, in a sense, concretely with virtues and vices, it represented much more graphically than did the Miracle Play the relationship between what a man *is* and what happens to him —in this case what "happens" being salvation or damnation.

In the *De Casibus*, or "Fall of Princes," tradition—at least in its sixteenth-century manifestations—there was also an emphatic correlation between cause and effect, between a man's nature and his fate. But here the context was almost exclusively human and mortal. The vice that led to destruction may have been Pride, the first of the Seven Deadly Sins, but it was usually represented in terms of contempt for human life, arrogance, brutality—sins not so much against the Holy Ghost as against man and society. And by the same token the penalty was a fall not in the next world but in this. Most important, the causal tie between sin and fall was not acted out by figures called Mankind and Pride and Death, but demonstrated in the lives of men called Julius Caesar and King Henry and the Duke of Buckingham. The system of analogies still operates, of course, and several of the collections of "Fall of Princes" stories begin with the story of Adam, whose fall is then seen as being re-enacted in the succeeding tales. The reality, however, lies not simply in the analogy, but in the dramatic theme itself. The men involved are not abstractions, nor distant quasi-mythological Biblical figures, but real and often virtually contemporary. Man is still a microcosm, but he is also *himself;* and the importance of the *De Casibus* tradition, apart from its subject matter and plot pattern, lies in its fusion of the universal with the individual and particular.

There is still another kind of reality that was in a sense indigenous to all native English drama, reality in a different and much more literal sense. Realism as a dramatic theory did not appear until the late nineteenth century; but the realism of physical violence, whether in the tricks and pratfalls of slapstick comedy or the slaughterhouse atmosphere—complete with pints of pigs' blood—of tragedy, has always been a conspicuous element on the English stage. This characteristic has sometimes been held up as a reproof to the English, as evidence either of their inherent bloodthirstiness or of their appalling lack of taste. In the case of the earlier drama, it has been excused on grounds of the crudity, if not outright barbarity, of the times. But in Elizabethan drama, and especially the plays of Shakespeare, this love of violence at times approaching savagery has been treated as an inexcusable blot in an otherwise sophisticated form of art. And it is perfectly true that physical violence is one of the earmarks of melodrama, which in itself is something less than the highest form of drama. But violence and brutality were very much a part of the reality of Elizabethan life. They lay just behind its façade of graciousness and sophistication—outside the walls of the Globe in Southwark, or in the dark alleys on the way home from the Blackfriars. Thus, while the settings and language of the stage might be anything but realistic, and the significant and "real" moral conflicts and dilemmas were acted out by figures from long ago or far away, the reality of violence provided a kind of tangible bond with the harsh world outside the theater. Doubtless the appeal of violence was in some cases purely sensational; and there are some plays that exploited this element beyond all bounds of either art or propriety. But while the appeal of gore and slapstick is anything but sophisticated, it was and is dramatically valid. Physical violence, in fun or deadly earnest, is a kind of immediate and concrete reminder that for all the grace and polish of our civilized virtues, in spite of the forms and formulas with which we have replaced savage directness, the elemental and brutal realities lie not far beneath the surface.

Finally, there was one sense of reality that Classical drama had

had in very highly developed form, and that in English drama was only fuzzily and incompletely seen before the advent of Greek and Roman models, a reality that can best be defined as aesthetic. English drama up through the early Elizabethan period was highly episodic, and while individual episodes might possess their own unity and integrity, plays as a whole were generally loosely constructed and ramshackle affairs. The Greek ideal of unified form, of a beginning, a middle, and an end, with an organic relationship between the parts and between form and content, was unknown, or at best dimly perceived. Coherence of language, of tone, of theme, or the notion that form is an integral part of both an intellectual and an aesthetic experience, are only some of the elements basic to Classical drama and largely absent in early English plays. The differences might be summed up by saying that early English drama did not look upon itself as an art form so much as a didactic device, a tool for teaching, or simply as casual entertainment. The Classical dramatist, on the other hand, saw his work as art, in the sense that it was an experience, not a lesson, and an experience that was determined by a consciously worked-out form. Once the English dramatists began to exploit, whether consciously or simply by imitation, this relationship between form and the dramatic experience, the great Elizabethan plays became possible.

Elizabethan drama, then, was more than simply a mechanical combination of conventions and techniques derived from the several contributory traditions; it was, at its best, a highly sophisticated art form that derived much of its range and durability from the complex and multi-level perception of "reality," perceptions that owed much to each of the diverse formative influences and yet were given unity and coherence by a strong sense of organic structure.

Needless to say, neither the feeling for structure nor the multiple representation of reality was achieved overnight, and some of the early attempts to find a workable fusion of the various available concepts of drama are laughable in their crudity. The

> A Lamentable Tragedy mixed full of pleasant mirth, containing
> The Life of Cambises, King of Persia—from the beginning of
> his kingdom, unto his death, his one good deed of execution,
> after that many wicked deeds and tyrannous murders, com-
> mitted by and through him, and last of all, his odious death by
> God's Justice appointed. Done in such order as followeth.

The dramatis personae of this strange hodgepodge is equally revealing, including the historical or quasi-historical figures Cambises, Smirdis, his brother, and Praxaspes, his counsellor; some
thoroughly English comic characters named Huf, Ruf, and Snuf,
who along with the rustics Hob and Lob, and Marian-May-Be-
Good, provide a slapstick subplot; Morality figures labeled
Shame, Diligence, Commons Complaint, Murder, and so on;
and, to round out the mélange, Venus and Cupid. What "follow-
eth" is an incredible mixture of low comedy, brutal tortures and
gory murders, pageantry, and morality, written in a species of
doggerel known as the "fourteener," a ballad meter, twelve hundred lines of which is enough to reduce a reasonably strong man
to gibbering frenzy. Obviously, everything is here, the panoramic
story demonstrating the reality of Moral Law, the violence and
slapstick of "real" life, the figures embodying human virtues and
vices, the fall of a prince who is blinded by pride, a touch of
Classical myth, and a poetic form. But the whole thing falls to
pieces; it is a totally incongruous jumble, because there is behind
it no coherent sense of the kind of reality it is trying to deal with.

Maturity: Elizabethan Tragedy and Comedy

It was Shakespeare—and this is one of the sources of his greatness—who most successfully fused the disparate elements that
made Elizabethan drama what it was and gave both vitality and

direction to a dramatic tradition that was in some danger of becoming lost in variety and confusion. But he was not the first of the great Elizabethan dramatists. Christopher Marlowe was Shakespeare's master, both in the sense that he broke the path that the greater genius was to follow, and because Shakespeare learned from him a great deal about the possibilities as well as the dangers of adapting the form of Classical tragedy to the popular theater. Just because he does represent a somewhat less sophisticated stage of development of the drama than Shakespeare, and because the range of his genius was more limited, Marlowe's plays reveal more distinctly some of the characteristic features of the handling of "reality" in Elizabethan drama.

Marlowe's *Dr. Faustus,* one of the finest of the pre-Shakespearean plays, appeared just twenty years after Preston's *Cambises* and is a revealing measure of how far dramatic art had matured in those all-important two decades. As a matter of fact, Marlowe's play contains almost exactly the same diverse elements from various sources that seemed so incongruous in *Cambises.* The later play is also a mixture of slapstick comedy, violence, pageantry, and didactic object lesson; the central character is conceived as historically "real"—at least to the extent that Cambises was; he is surrounded by Morality figures, most obviously in the pageant of the Seven Deadly Sins, but also in the Good and Bad Angels and in Mephistophilis; the comic episodes introduce English rustics, such as Robin and Ralph; and Classical mythology enters in the figure of Helen of Troy. But far from being the conglomeration of unrelated fragments that *Cambises* is, *Dr. Faustus* is held together both by a carefully controlled form, in its plot and in its language, and by a coherent vision of reality.

In thematic concerns, too, *Dr. Faustus'* debts to earlier traditions are obvious. The treatment is panoramic, covering in a series of episodes twenty-four years of a man's life; and while the subject is hardly Biblical, the story is a "real" demonstration of a spiritual truth. The implicit but central reality of the play, although it is denied by Faustus himself, lies at the heart of Christian faith, the reality of Divine Grace. The Morality element is apparent not only in the characters but in the fact that the play concerns primarily the proper conduct of a man's life, and the consummation of that life in salvation or damnation. Indeed, Heaven and Hell are the omnipresent poles of the play, providing the central conflict and dramatic tension.

Although Faustus is no prince, he is a prince of scholars, having risen as high in the fields of learning as the academic disciplines of his day permitted, and the pattern of the play is that of the *De Casibus* tradition. Faustus, driven by pride, ambition, a desire for power—an unwillingness to be "but Faustus, and a man"—would defy the limitations of humanity and be more than man. To gain this end he binds himself, not to the Wheel of Fortune, exactly, but to its theological counterpart, the Devil. With his magical powers he rises, literally, to superhuman heights of power and fame, but in the end he is hurled down, not just to mortal ruin but to eternal ruin. In fact, Faustus' life is a retelling of the ultimate "Fall" story, that of Lucifer.

Finally, we have in *Dr. Faustus* the artistic unity of a closely knit form and structure. Although the early editions of the play, in common with most Elizabethan dramas, lacked act and scene divisions, it falls easily into the conventional five-act pattern regularized by the Romans. More important, the play has a clearly defined beginning, middle, and end. The beginning encompasses Faustus' speeches of dissatisfaction with his mortal limitations, and the temptation to magic, and culminates in his signing of the bond with Lucifer. The middle of the play traces the consequences of his act, representing on the one hand the ways in which he uses his powers and on the other the effect of these powers on his personality. And the end reveals the last day of Faustus' life before the terms of his pact are consummated.

The unity of *Dr. Faustus* lies, however, not simply in more or less mechanical matters of structure but in more subtle aspects of form, such as language. Although Marlowe was writing in the somewhat bombastic rhetorical tradition of the early Elizabethan period, his genius is nowhere more evident than in the skill with which he molds the rhythms and sound of his blank verse not only to the content of a speech but to the state of mind he wishes to represent. Look, for instance, at some of Faustus' speeches early in the play, when he is in the full flower of his pride, speeches such as those beginning:

> How am I glutted with conceit of this!
> Shall I make spirits fetch me what I please,
> Resolve me of all ambiguities,
> Perform what desperate enterprise I will? (I.i.77–80)[1]

or

> Had I as many souls as there be stars,
> I'd give them all for Mephistophilis.
> By him I'll be great Emperor of the world . . . (I.iii106–108)

In these and other early speeches the regular, almost unbroken march of the rhythm and the rich combinations of sounds effectively suggest both the grandiose ambitions and the supreme self-assurance of this man who would be as a god. Or again, the famous speech to Helen, beginning, "Was this the face that launch'd a thousand ships,/ And burnt the topless towers of Ilium?," while not so regular, reflects in rhythms and breathless exclamations the excitement, indeed the passionate obsession, of the speaker with the sensual joys Helen represents. And nothing reveals so poignantly the distance Faustus has come from the proud and self-confident scholar of the early speeches than the halting, irregular, panic-stricken rhythms of his final soliloquy:

> O, I'll leap up to my God! Who pulls me down?
> See, see where Christ's blood streams in the firmament!
> One drop would save my soul—half a drop: ah, my Christ!

[1] In the case of most English and American plays, which are readily available in a variety of reliable editions, the source of quotations will be indicated by reference in the text to the generally accepted act and scene divisions. *Doctor Faustus* is, however, something of a special case, since there are several different "accepted" ways of dividing the play. The references here will be to the text in *Elizabethan Plays,* ed. Hazelton Spencer (Boston: Little, Brown and Co., 1933).

Concepts of Reality in the Great Periods of Drama

Ah, rend not my heart for naming of my Christ!
Yet I will call on him: O spare me, Lucifer!—
Where is it now? 'Tis gone; and see where God
Stretcheth out his arm, and bends his ireful brows! (V.ii.90–96)

Many critics have found a serious source of *dis*unity in *Dr. Faustus* in the long and admittedly sometimes tedious "comic" episodes in the middle of the play, as well as the repeated intrusions of various rustics and clowns. It is true that these episodes break the otherwise unrelieved solemnity of the play; but English drama has from its beginning mixed serious and comic elements, as does life. And these often rather crude episodes of slapstick comedy are not simply irrelevant "comic relief"—but an organic part of the structure of the play.

The scene between Wagner and the Clown early in the play is a good illustration. The episode falls between Faustus' promise to Mephistophilis—that he will sell his soul to Lucifer in exchange for magical powers—and the actual signing of the bond. In it the Clown, impressed by Wagner's power over some minor devils, sells himself as a bond servant in return for a "shoulder of mutton," a piece of gold, and the magic power to turn himself into a flea so that he may "tickle the wenches." The bargain is a mock one, to be sure, but in the context the mockery is indirectly aimed at Faustus. The scene reduces his actions to the level of the vulgar and ridiculous, and fine-sounding statements of intention to the level of mere self-indulgence. One is forced to ask the question: Is what Faustus wants really so much superior to what the Clown wants? There is bitter irony, however, in the fact that the Clown's contract is for seven years, Faustus' forever.

The comic episodes in the middle of the play differ somewhat in various early editions, but all editions have in common the scenes at the palace of the Pope, Faustus' tricking of the "horse-courser," and the episode in which he brings grapes to the Duchess of Vanholt. These are relevant not because of analogies with the main action but as part *of* the main action. In these scenes we see exactly how Faustus makes use of his great powers, exactly how far he lives up to the fine promises he made before

114   the powers were actually his. Here, with his paltry practical jokes on the Pope, the petty revenge on the horse-courser, the sleight-of-hand with the grapes, we see the great scholar, who with super-human powers would ring all Germany with brass and drive the Prince of Parma from his land, reduced to the level of a parlor magician. Absolute power, it would seem, corrupts absolutely —and however magnificent in his pride and defiance Faustus may have seemed at the beginning of the play, his character and his stature have collapsed completely.

However much the structure of the action or the skillful use of language contribute to the artistic coherence of *Dr. Faustus,* it is ultimately the intense and almost exclusive focus on a single domi-nant personality that gives the play its formal and thematic unity. This "one-man" quality, which is characteristic of Marlowe's work, is not necessarily a virtue. Better plays before and since have lacked this element. But it is such a striking characteristic that the "reality" of the play can best be discussed in terms of it.

Everything in *Dr. Faustus* bears either directly or indirectly upon our understanding of the personality of its hero, his inner conflict—or at least dilemma—and the consequences of his choice. Within the framework of the play Faustus is of course an individual, with a unique education and abnormally developed ambition and drive. But at the same time he is representative of *all* men, in their dissatisfaction with their limitations as human beings, in their unwillingness to stand still and accept passively whatever place in life fate has chosen for them, in their perfectly human desire to be "more than man." Similarly, the figures that surround Faustus and pull him in one direction or another can be taken literally, within the dramatic context, as concrete agents of Heaven and Hell; but they also represent the two conflicting forces of human nature, within Faustus and in man in general. The Good and Bad Angels, for instance, can be seen simply as a dramatic projection, after the fashion of expressionism several centuries later, of two sides of Faustus' nature struggling for dominance, his conscience and his baser desires, his spiritual and his animal natures.

Concepts of Reality in the Great Periods of Drama

Even Mephistophilis can be taken as a reflection of something *within* Faustus. It is significant that Mephistophilis does not come of his own accord, but only when Faustus has abjured God and the Trinity and prayed to Lucifer. And Mephistophilis does not tempt Faustus—indeed, at one point he urges him to turn back. It is Faustus who lists all the rewards he hopes to get in exchange for his soul, and it is Faustus who spells out the terms of the contract. There is no "outside" force of evil luring Faustus on or coercing him in any way. In a very real sense he both tempts himself and damns himself. Similarly, later in the play, the Helen to whom Faustus willingly gives up his soul in exchange for an "immortal kiss" is only a spirit, a figment conjured up by Faustus himself out of nothing.

In much the same way, the contract that Faustus makes with Lucifer is a particular and literal document and at the same time symbolic of all defiance of Divine Law, of the assumption by *any* man that he is above the limitations placed on other men; and, in a larger sense, it is symbolic of any consciously wrongful act by which we hope to gain power or pleasure for ourselves. All men rationalize in favor of what they want at the expense of what they know is right; and the degree to which Faustus blinds himself to what he knows to be true is significant. Early in the play there is a revealing piece of logic whereby Faustus convinces himself that what "will be, shall be," and that therefore magic is no worse than anything else in a world predestined to damnation. That this doctor of theology should in his syllogism casually skip over the whole concept of Grace on which Christianity is based shows much about his state of mind. And throughout the play he persistently denies the authority of God or the reality of Hell while at the same time accepting as "real"—because the source of his powers—the Devil. This is a logical contradiction that a confirmed atheist would hoot at. But Faustus, who would be as a god himself, cannot accept the reality of an omnipotent God, Who by definition represents a limitation of his powers, and still get what he wants; so he must blind himself to what he knows to be true.

Elizabethan Drama

Moreover, what happens to Faustus is also both particular and universal. The damnation with which the play ends is of course intended to be taken literally; but it is also symbolic. Early in the play Mephistophilis suggests that damnation is not simply a place, but a state or condition of mind:

> Why this is hell, nor am I out of it.
> Think'st thou that I, who saw the face of God,
> And tasted the eternal joys of Heaven,
> Am not tormented with ten thousand hells
> In being deprived of everlasting bliss?   (I.iii.80–84)

And in this sense Faustus is damned even before the devils carry him off screaming to Hell Mouth. In signing his bond with Lucifer, and indeed throughout the whole play, Faustus, as we have seen, must deny that there is any God above him, because to admit his dependence is incompatible with his aspirations. But in denying that there is anything above or outside himself and his desires that gives life meaning, Faustus has deprived his life of all meaning. Having denied a higher God, there is nothing left but himself; and as Faustus says, "The God thou serv'st is thine own appetite." It is for this reason that all his fine altruistic promises as to how he will put his powers to use to serve his country, his university, his fellow students, come to nothing, and his powers are reduced to mere self-indulgence. Indeed, in his passionate speech to the ghost of Helen, he can say, "For love of thee,/ Instead of Troy, shall Wittenberg be sack'd." With nothing to live for but himself, he does just that. But the meaning of spiritual isolation from God, and of a life given over to passing pleasures and amusement, comes home to Faustus as he is forced by its immediacy to contemplate the price he must pay.

In the final soliloquy we see a very different and rather frightening Faustus. He does not repent, because he does not know how; he is only terrified at what has happened to him. Having for twenty-four years acknowledged no other god but his own appetite, he has forgotten how to speak to any other. The man who once aspired to be more than man now begs Fate to

make him less than man—an animal, a stone, a drop of water.
Faustus has learned what humanity means by denying his own;
he has learned that man is man because he is not a god, because
he has limitations; but the price of this knowledge is that, far
from becoming superhuman, he becomes subhuman, a devil.

Faustus' fate is, we may hope, not a universal one; but the man
himself is representative of man's dual nature and impulses, and
what happens to him is a universal possibility: the triumph of
the purely selfish and animal. The reality of the play, achieved
through the co-ordination of such elements as the characterization of Faustus, the structure of the action, the language, the
symbolic analogies with human experience, might be defined,
then, as the relationship between the individual and the spiritual
and moral universe.

Another way of coming to understand the particular "realism"
of the Elizabethan theater is to project ourselves in imagination
into its audience and try to see the reality they would have seen.
And it might be fruitful to use this kind of approach with one of
Shakespeare's plays, for although he learned much from Marlowe, his work represents a significant advance in complexity and
sophistication. Shakespeare's plays are in themselves ample
evidence that the double burden of providing unity and embodying or representing "reality'" need not be shouldered by a single
central character. It is true that there is usually one powerful
and dominant figure, a Macbeth or a King Lear, but he is surrounded by other well-developed characters. Shakespeare's stage
is richer, more crowded with personalities, than was Marlowe's,
and his protagonists more complex and multifaceted than
Faustus.

The differences between the two dramatists were not so great,
however, as to have surprised or confused their audiences, who
would simply have seen Shakespeare as "another playwright"
writing in the same tradition as the much-esteemed Marlowe. Of
course, Shakespeare developed tremendously in the course of
his productive life, and so did his audience. But even at his ma-

turity, in *King Lear* say, he is writing within the context of conventions that are still much the same as they were in Marlowe's time, and so is his concept of reality.

Using *King Lear* (1606) for illustrations, since it is one of Shakespeare's most mature and complex plays, we might ask ourselves what kind of reality his audience would have looked for—and found.

One quality the Elizabethan audience would have neither anticipated nor seen was any kind of visual realism. The costumes were contemporary, not historical; and the stage, as it had always been in England, was bare, except for a minimum of essential stage props—a chair and table, perhaps, a set of stocks for Kent to sit in, a wine cup, but little more. The "real" location of the action was indicated casually in the dialogue, or sometimes simply by *who* was speaking. If a more elaborate sense of the physical setting was necessary, it was provided by the poetry itself. So Lear's speech on the heath replaced all the flashing lights, shaken tin, and wind machines of the later theater:

> Blow, winds, and crack your cheeks! rage! blow!
> You cataracts and hurricanoes, spout
> Till you have drench'd our steeples, drown'd the cocks!
> You sulph'rous and thought-executing fires,
> Vaunt-couriers to oak-cleaving thunderbolts,
> Singe my white head! And thou, all-shaking thunder,
> Strike flat the thick rotundity o' th' world . . . (III.ii.1–7)

A play of Shakespeare's, after all, in common with all so-called "imaginative" literature, is not only a product of the imagination but depends on the imagination for its effect. And Lear's speeches can create a more powerful sense of violent turmoil both within and without the speaker than can any amount of stage machinery. In another play, *Henry V* (*ca.* 1600), Shakespeare drops all pretense and appeals directly and explicitly to the imaginations of his audience, but only because of the extraordinary demands he plans to make on them:

> . . . Pardon, gentles all,
> The flat unraised spirits that have dar'd

Concepts of Reality in the Great Periods of Drama

On this unworthy scaffold to bring forth
So great an object. Can this cockpit hold
The vasty fields of France? Or may we cram
Within this wooden O the very casques
That did affright the air at Agincourt?
O, pardon! . . .
And let us, ciphers to this great accompt,
On your imaginary forces work.
Suppose within the girdle of these walls
Are now confin'd two mighty monarchies,
Whose high-upreared and abutting fronts
The perilous narrow ocean parts asunder.
Piece out our imperfections with your thoughts:
Into a thousand parts divide one man
And make imaginary puissance.
Think, when we talk of horses, that you see them
Printing their proud hoofs i' th' receiving earth.
For 'tis your thoughts that now must deck our kings,
Carry them here and there, jumping o'er times,
Turning th' accomplishment of many years
Into an hourglass. (Prologue. 8–31)

In any realistic production such an obvious pointing to the illusion of the theater would, necessarily, ruin the illusion. But where there is no pretense of mirroring literal reality, nothing is damaged but the possibility of unconvincing fakery when the playwright frankly turns to his audience and begs them to "eke out our performance with your mind." Explicitly or implicitly, all the Elizabethans did this—and in our own day Thornton Wilder's Stage Manager in *Our Town* is a modern version of Shakespeare's Chorus-Prologue. And in all cases, such open acknowledgment that the play exists not so much in the real world as in the world of the imagination only serves to expand, rather than contract, the area of "suspension of disbelief."

The relationship between the play and the audience evident in Shakespeare's use of the Chorus, just cited, is implicit in other stage conventions of the age. The soliloquies and frequent asides, often addressed directly to the crowd, and the apron stage itself, reaching out into the audience, all suggest a curiously ambivalent relationship. The stage was not *apart* from the audience, as it has

120   tended to be since the introduction of the proscenium arch or "picture frame" stage, nor was it a part of "everyday life." It lay somewhere in between, just as the play itself lay somewhere between factual reality and purely imaginative fantasy—not belonging to either, but partaking of both. The proximity of the stage and the audience, the interplay and intimacy between them, far from being a violation of the dramatic experience, was very much a part of it.

The aural, or verbal, realism of Elizabethan drama follows much the same pattern, and there is no consistent effort to make the dialogue sound like an actual conversation outside the theater. Even though Elizabethan spoken English seems to have been closer to the rhythms and color of poetry than it is today, the language of *King Lear* to a contemporary audience was manifestly poetry and not everyday speech. This fact is sometimes overlooked by modern actors who consciously but mistakenly try to make Shakespeare sound as flat and unpoetic as possible, and in so doing miss the whole point of Elizabethan drama.

The use of poetic rather than prosaic language served several functions directly related to the kind of reality the plays concerned. For one thing, poetry is infinitely richer and, with its highly figurative language, its rhythms and unusual verbal patterns, can both stimulate the imagination and control nuances of emphasis and tone to a degree impossible with the casual and careless language of the streets. Of course, the essence of poetry *is* its figurative language, its metaphors and similes and comparisons; and the virtue of figurative language is that it can mean and suggest so much more than it *says*. It can, as in Lear's speech quoted earlier, not only describe an objective fact (the storm) but also suggest a state of mind. Indeed, a metaphor is a kind of bridge between an objective fact and an attitude or moral vision —because of the *kind* of comparison made. By personifying the storm as a kind of malignant spirit ("Blow, winds, and crack your cheeks!") to whom he is issuing commands ("Crack Nature's moulds, all germains spill at once,/ That make ingrateful man!"), Lear becomes identified with the storm and with the bitterness, the uncurbed violence, the moral incoherence that he sees in *it,* but which we are led to see in *him* and in the human world around him, as well as in the natural world.

The metaphor, because by its nature it suggests comparisons, opens out, as it were, not only in the direction of particular analogies and parallels but in the direction of universal implication. The metaphoric relationship between Lear and the storm not only illuminates the old king's spiritual state but, because of the language he uses about the storm, suggests a chaos that at least temporarily engulfs the world and indeed the universe. It is through metaphoric language, then, that a particular thing or fact, in this case the storm, is endowed with larger implication and meaning. In much this sense, a play is itself a kind of metaphor, an imaginative parallel or analogy to life, by which human nature and actions are endowed with a new significance and meaning. In a way, the metaphors of poetic drama *are* the reality with which it deals.

To put it another way, the poetic language of Elizabethan drama serves to define the area of reality—that of poetry and poetic truth. And this is perhaps the aspect of early drama most frequently misunderstood by the modern reader, conditioned to the literalism of the contemporary theater. Many students, confronted with an interpretation of a Shakespeare play based on patterns of imagery, subtleties of tone, sound patterns, ambiguities of meaning and nuances of suggestion, will throw up their hands in horror and ask, "How do you know Shakespeare *intended* all that?"—and yet are perfectly willing to accept the same devices as part of the natural language of poetry. But to Shakespeare and the other Elizabethans drama was simply a subdivision of poetry, and the techniques and effects of one were taken as natural to the other. Poetry, in other words, far from being mere decoration, is the heart of Elizabethan drama; it defines its reality and, like the bare stage, removes it from the realm of the literal and everyday to the level of the poetic and imaginative and metaphoric.

If Shakespeare's audience would not even have noticed the

absence of visual or verbal realism, those being irrelevant to what they expected from a play, what kind of reality would they have found? They would have appreciated, for one thing, a rather vague sense of historical authenticity. The story of Lear and his daughters was one of the legends of ancient Britain that had been handed down from the distant past, and they might have read it in one of various printed versions or have been familiar with an earlier play on the subject. And there would have been a pleasant sense that they were witnessing an incident out of their own national history. But much more important than the knowledge that it *did* happen was the feeling that it *could* happen.

And the sense that it could happen depended on the fact that the audience saw in the moral qualities embodied in the various characters, and in the causal connection between what a person was and what happened to him, a reflection of a moral order that they at least believed they saw in the real world. It would be a gross oversimplification to see the characters in *King Lear* as mere allegorical figures. They are certainly not represented as abstractions, or even as such relatively simple, one-dimensional humans as Faustus. But at the same time, the Morality Play tradition, with its practice of embodying specific moral traits in particular characters, which was so important in Marlowe's play, still exists in Shakespeare's plays. Lear himself is a personification of pride—although in a significant break with the Morality tradition he ends the play not as Pride, but as Humility. And Lear is surrounded by characters in whom a single virtue or vice is all-important. Kent and Edgar represent political and filial loyalty respectively. Edmund, the illegitimate son, might have been labeled Lawlessness or Rebellion. Goneril and Regan are embodiments of filial *dis*loyalty, although their ruling passion seems to be avarice. And Cordelia, for all her silence, is Love.

There is nothing to be gained by exaggerating this "allegorical" element in *King Lear,* but it is there, the audience would certainly have expected to find it, and it is very much, as we shall see, a part of the reality of the play.

King Lear, like *Dr. Faustus,* is concerned with the relationship between the individual and the moral universe. The difference is that the moral universe is not represented directly, through Good and Bad Angels, a contract with the Devil, visions of Heaven and Hell, but as it is embodied in human beings. The moral conflict is not stated explicitly in terms of salvation and damnation, nor is the moral responsibility of the individual seen in terms of the acceptance or denial of God, but as a relationship with other humans. Lear, like Faustus, is unable to accept at the beginning the limitations of his humanity; but while he is still to be seen in a moral framework, his story is acted out in the context of *this* world and the complex human and social relations that exist in it.

On the simplest level—and this is doubtless where most of the audience would have seen it—*King Lear* is the story of a proud old king who, as one of his daughters says of him, "hath ever but slenderly known himself" and in the blindness of his pride makes some costly mistakes in judgment. He wants to give up the authority and responsibilities of the crown to his three daughters but thinks to retain its honors and prerogatives; and more important, he misjudges the three recipients. More specifically, Lear's errors fall into three relatively distinct categories: First, there is his political folly. For the Elizabethan with his strong sense of both the rights and the obligations of a monarch, Lear's plan to retain one while giving up the other would have seemed a direct denial of his divinely ordained responsibilities. And to the English people, politically united for the first time and glorying in their sense of national identity, the proposed tripartite division of the country would have seemed political suicide.

Lear betrays his responsibility not only to the state but to the family. In rejecting Cordelia's honesty and in disinheriting her, he violates the bonds that hold the family together; and he does so because he completely misunderstands the nature of those bonds. Love is for him something bought and sold; it is Cordelia's ability to "heave her heart into her mouth" to flatter him and buy a "third more opulent than her sisters."

Elizabethan Drama

Finally, Lear allows his passions to overcome completely his rational powers. In the fury of his hurt pride he cannot understand the truth of what Cordelia tries to tell him; and his response to Kent's wisdom is to banish him, and thereby "kill his physician."

In other words, Lear can be said to have violated the political, the familial, and the rational order. But more basically, he violates order itself, the bonds that hold things together and are a stay against chaos. And as a consequence of the violation, chaos does reign in each of the areas mentioned. In the political realm there is disintegration, rebellion, and ultimately invasion. In familial relationships, the daughters turn on their father and thrust him out into the raging storm, and Gloucester's son turns on his father and destroys him. And in the rational world there is, of course, madness. It is as if Lear's sin, if it can be called that, his pride and presumption and blindness, provided, in his own words, the first crack in "Nature's moulds," and with the breaking of order the ordered universe collapses.

Probably few words appear as often in this play as the term *Nature,* and it is worth saying something about its implications. It seems to have two diametrically opposed meanings. There is nature in the sense used above, where it is associated with a mold or pattern, the ordered nature of reason and morality, rights and obligations, law and humanity. It is to this nature that Lear ironically appeals ("Hear, Nature, hear!") in his prayer of vengeance against his *undutiful* daughters. But there is another kind of nature, the nature of tooth and claw, of irrationality and passion, of disobedience and rebellion, of illegitimacy and brutality. It is the nature to which the *"natural"* (Elizabethan term for illegitimate) son Edmund appeals in his long soliloquy beginning, "Thou, Nature, art my goddess," and ending, "Now, gods, stand up for bastards!" (I.ii.1-22).

As a consequence of Lear's violation of the natural order (in the first sense), the world of brutal and amoral nature at least for a time achieves complete ascendancy. The play is filled with metaphors of order turned upside down and bestiality triumphant over what is rational and human, but perhaps the most pointed is the Fool's jibe at Lear: "When thou clovest thy crown i' th' middle and gav'st away both parts, thou bor'st thine ass on thy back o'er the dirt" (I.iv.174-177). The ultimate *symbol* of disorder is, of course, the storm.

In the midst of the chaos he has both literally and metaphorically brought about, and to a degree because of it, Lear begins, only dimly at first, to see where he had not seen before. The violence of the storm brings him out of himself, to think for the first time of his responsibilities to others:

> O, I have ta'en
> Too little care of this! Take physic, pomp;
> Expose thyself to feel what wretches feel,
> That thou mayst shake the superflux to them
> And show the heavens more just. (III.iv.28–36)

However, it is only when he has passed through the purgatory of madness, the "sulph'rous and thought-executing fires" of the *mind's* storm, that Lear achieves even a metaphoric recognition of his own blindness:

> They flatter'd me like a dog, and told me I had white hairs in my beard ere the black ones were there. To say 'ay' and 'no' to everything I said! 'Ay' and 'no' too was no good divinity. When the rain came to wet me once, and the wind to make me chatter; when the thunder would not peace at my bidding; there I found 'em, there I smelt 'em out. Go to, they are not men o' their words! They told me I was everything. 'Tis a lie—I am not ague-proof. (IV.vi.98–107)

But Lear's return to order and health is not achieved by suffering alone; he has one daughter "who redeems nature from the general curse/ Which twain have brought her to" (IV.vi.209-211). It is Cordelia and the love she represents that "cure this great breach in . . . abused nature" (IV.vii.15), by demonstrating to her father a love that is based not on flattery and self-interest but on humility and mutuality.

In the end the natural order of love and loyalty, reason and law, which has never been destroyed but only driven underground, is once more in the ascendant. Political order is restored, and at least momentarily Lear is once again on the throne of a united country, his family is restored in his acceptance of Cordelia and her forgiveness of him, and he is once more sane. Order has been regained, but only at a price, and all is not necessarily happy. The damage has been done; Lear cannot turn the clock back and say he's sorry he was so stupid. An ordered nature has been re-affirmed, but at human cost—the cost of Lear and Cordelia.

This has been a much oversimplified summary of the play, but it should make clear the basic moral as well as artistic pattern. In a sense, the play *has* a pattern and is *about* a pattern, and this is the reality of the play. The subject of *King Lear* is a moral, natural, political order in the world, and it is made tangible, as it were, through a form: the poetic language, the patterns of the action, the characterization. The traits represented by Lear, Edmund, Cordelia, and the others are real human characteristics, and their interaction and consequences in the play reflect an order in "real" life.

It might be added that the order and pattern given to life and experience by a play such as *King Lear,* or by any work by art, do not represent something new *created* by the work. It has been said that to understand something we have to know it already. Shakespeare, then, was simply using his art to bring into focus a reality his audience already knew and in a sense *expected* to find.

Although Shakespeare's plays offer a representative example of the kind of reality we can expect to find in Elizabethan drama in general, he was virtually unique in the broad range and universality of that reality—which is the point made by Jonson in his well-known words of praise: "He was not of an age but for all time." Marlowe's *Dr. Faustus,* as we have seen, although the techniques were in some ways very similar to Shakespeare's, deals with a much narrower range of human experience and spiritual truth, however significant that may be in itself.

The playwrights who followed Shakespeare, too, seem to be satisfied with a much more circumscribed perception or range of reality. In the tragicomedy of the period, because of its un-

believable characterization and arbitrary action, we can legitimately question whether there is in fact a view of life or human
nature that has any reasonable relevance to a "real" moral or
human world. But even tragedy seems to degenerate in terms of
its grasp of any meaningful reality. *The Revenger's Tragedy*
(1607), usually attributed to Cyril Tourneur, is an extreme example of one characteristic tendency of the period. The characters are largely one-dimensional representatives of specific
virtues and vices and still bear Morality Play labels, thinly disguised by their Italianate forms; and the action of the play is
wholly incredible. But these defects are not truly important in
terms of what the play is about. The burden of "reality" in the
play is carried almost entirely by the language, which is rich,
almost sensuous, in its rhythms and magnificent in its metaphors
of corruption and death. Both the spirit and the technique of the
play are epitomized in one of its best-known speeches. Vendice,
the protagonist, is addressing the skull of his late mistress:

> And now methinks I could e'en chide myself
> For doating on her beauty, though her death
> Shall be revenged after no common action.
> Does the silkworm expend her yellow labours
> For thee? For thee does she undo herself?
> Are lordships sold to maintain ladyships,
> For the poor benefit of a bewildering minute?
> Why does yon fellow falsify highways,
> And put his life between the judge's lips,
> To refine such a thing—keeps horse and men
> To beat their valours for her?
>
>   *   *   *
>
> Does every proud and self-affecting dame
> Camphire her face for this, and grieve her Maker
> In sinful baths of milk, when many an infant starves
> For her superfluous outside—all for this?
> Who now bids twenty pounds a night? All are hushed.
> Thou may'st lie chaste now! it were fine, methinks,
> To have thee seen at revels, forgetful feasts,
> And unclean brothels! sure, 'twould fright the sinner,
> Out of his antic amble,
> And cloy an epicure with empty dishes. (III.iv)

Elizabethan Drama

128   This is fine stuff! Probably there are few more effective representations of the transience of both life and physical beauty. And unquestionably there is nothing more real than death. This notion, along with a sense of the ubiquity of moral corruption, provides the substance and theme of the play. But real though they may be, death and depravity are far from being the only reality; and to represent them as such involves a distinct distortion of human experience. Tourneur, and indeed many of his contemporaries, can fairly be accused of relying for their effects on mere sensationalism.

There is no need to describe here the work of the other dramatists who followed Shakespeare in the early seventeenth century—the somewhat more controlled morbidity of Webster or the psychological probings into abnormal moral states of Ford. It is enough to say that after about 1610 the artistic impulse and the firm grasp on a meaningful and universal reality that characterized the early Elizabethans, and especially Marlowe and Shakespeare, seem to dwindle and wither away. There are individual plays that reveal superb poetry, or penetrating character analysis, or skillfully worked out plots; occasionally a particular and narrow aspect of reality is effectively captured on the stage. But rarely do we feel that a significant and timeless perception of the human condition has suddenly achieved reality in dramatic form.

Something does, however, need to be said about Elizabethan comedy, which has been ignored here not because it is unimportant but because much of what has been said about reality in tragedy could, with some modifications, be said also about comedy. As has been suggested before, the *attitude* of comedy toward reality is very different, but the reality itself, and the way in which it is represented, may be very much the same as in tragedy.

In Shakespeare's romantic comedy *Twelfth Night* (1602), the characters themselves are too far exaggerated and distorted to be realistic. As in *King Lear,* the reality lies in the relationships between the virtues and follies represented by the various characters, and between the possession of certain qualities and their consequences in the action. Malvolio, for example, can be seen as a kind of comic Lear, for he too "hath ever but slenderly known himself." He is master of a household he cannot control, blinded as he is by self-love: "So cramm'd, as he thinks, with excellencies that it is his grounds of faith that all that look on him love him" (II.iii.163–165). But the consequence of his blindness is a purely comic "rebellion," a largely farcical period of "suffering" in which he is brought to the point of pleading that he is just as much "in his wits" as the Fool.

The showing up of Malvolio of course occupies only part of *Twelfth Night;* but the self-delusions of Orsino and Olivia are largely responsible for the confusion and disorder that it is the business of the rest of the play to develop and then resolve. This play, like *King Lear,* has two plots, distinct and yet related in terms of both characters and theme; and it is the common ground between the plots—the investigation of the varieties of self-delusion that grow out of misdirected love—that the play is *about.* The theme is developed through a vast amount of fooling—in a variety of senses; but folly is, after all, just as real as tragic blindness.

While the physical setting of *Twelfth Night* is as far from being representational as that of *King Lear,* it might be argued that the language, because it is largely prose, *is* more realistic. But the sustained wit, the clever repartee, the comic banter of comedy are no more the language of everyday life than is the highly metaphoric speech of poetry. In a sense, the language of wit removes comedy from the commonplace "realistic" world just as effectively as the poetry of tragedy. But, appropriately, the level of reality to which we are moved is not that of poetic and universal truths, not to a confrontation of the ultimate ambiguities and mysteries of existence, but to an *intellectual* perception of human limitations. Poetry and tragedy give coherence and order to the baffling and incomprehensible aspects of human nature and experience by suggesting that they are part of a dimly seen and intuitively acknowledged pattern. Wit and comedy create an analogous sense of ordering experience by suggesting that what can be understood can be controlled. The mysteries and paradoxes of life become the surprises and incongruities of comedy, and witty language is a mark of comprehension. As we have already seen, tragedy is characteristically concerned with the elements in man's nature or his place in the universe that are beyond his control and perhaps even his understanding, and must therefore be accepted; comedy is usually concerned with what can be controlled by man—and wit is the tangible evidence of that control.

Comedy, consequently, does not usually treat man's ultimate situation but his follies and, specifically, his human and social relationships. The reality of comedy, then, is perhaps not so much what man *is* as what he ought to be, as determined by his social peers. Ben Jonson, Shakespeare's friend and contemporary, and one of the greatest writers of Elizabethan plays, wrote a species of comedy in which the virtues and follies are very distinctly seen in social terms.

Satire is comedy that holds some deviation from a norm, whether moral or social, up to ridicule, and satire was Jonson's natural language. His plays, like so much Elizabethan drama, owe a very obvious debt to the Morality tradition, in that his characters are very distinctly typed. That is, each exhibits only a single dominant characteristic, which is usually identified by his name. There is, however, this important difference: The one-sidedness of Morality characters is not itself an object of ridicule, because they are by their nature abstractions and not to be judged in terms of "real" persons. In satire such as Jonson's this one-sidedness *is* ridiculous, because there is at least an implicit norm of the rational, well-balanced human personality. In this sense, the frame of reference in Jonson's comedy—that of contemporary London society—is much more literally realistic than in the Morality tradition itself.

In some of Jonson's plays the norm—the values in terms of which we judge the characters—is explicitly moral. In what is probably his best-known satire, *Volpone* (1606), Voltore (vulture), Corbaccio (crow), Volpone (fox), and the rest of the menagerie become *in*human because of their single-minded, even depraved greed, rapaciousness, lust, and jealousy—qualities suggestive of the Seven Deadly Sins. Even so, these are treated as social vices—they harm others and break down the proper relationships of society, and the consequences are represented as social penalties, loss of wealth, the scorn of one's peers, or, in the case of Volpone and Mosca, the judgment of society's instrument, the law court.

In Jonson's "humor" comedy the norm is even more specifically social. The notion of the humors goes back to a medieval theory of psychology according to which a man's temperament and personality are determined by the balance or imbalance of certain substances, "hot," "cold," "wet," and "dry," in his physiological make-up. As Jonson uses the term, however, a humor not only implies an oddity or extravagance in the personality but suggests something of a pose, a hobbyhorse, or a fad that a person follows because he thinks it is the thing to do. In humor comedy, then, the vices tend to be social follies, and the punishment is exposure to the laughter of the rest of society. There is, in other words, one significant sense in which satire, and comedy in general, differs from Shakespearean or Marlovian tragedy in its perception of reality: Reality lies not so much in the moral law of God as in the social law of man—and the implicit norm is conformity to an ideal social pattern.

This specification of Shakespearean and Marlovian tragedy is necessary because, as we have seen, tragedy after Shakespeare tended to become narrower and more social in its concerns. Indeed, after the first decade of the seventeenth century both tragedy and comedy became increasingly limited in their range. One of the reasons for this is that, for various economic and social reasons, the drama was becoming more and more the exclusive property of a small and aristocratic class. The playwrights wrote more and more for the audiences in the higher priced, socially restricted "private" theaters in the city and less for the popular theaters in the suburbs or across the river. What developed as a result was essentially "coterie" drama, based on

132   the special tastes and values of a particular class, and often snobbish in its treatment of other classes—specifically, the rising middle class of merchants and businessmen. It tended to be cynical, sensational in a somewhat intellectual way, and to indulge in the "private joke." Reality, in this kind of situation, becomes the reality of a very limited and specialized group of people— and hence runs the danger of being no reality at all. Cut off from the broad base of popular theater, drama during the reign of Charles the First dwindled into farce and melodrama, and when the theaters were officially closed by act of Parliament in 1642, because of the civil disorders associated with the Puritan rebellion, nothing much was lost that was not already dying.

SUGGESTIONS FOR READING

Dr. Faustus is unique, and none of Marlowe's other plays would make an adequate substitute. *Tamburlaine* (*ca.* 1587), however, offers another approach to the Promethean hero. *Edward II* (*ca.* 1593), in some ways Marlowe's best play, is entirely different in both style and subject matter.

Much of what is said here about *King Lear* could be adapted to apply to Shakespeare's other mature tragedies, such as *Macbeth* (*ca.* 1610) or *Othello* (1604). *Hamlet* (*ca.* 1600), however, is so complex and so debatable that it offers rather unsure ground for any generalizations about the playwright's methods; and *Antony and Cleopatra* (*ca.* 1607), while one of the best, presents some special problems in its denouement that are outside the present discussion.

The "decadent" drama of Jacobean and Caroline England is best represented by *Sejanus* (Jonson, 1603), *The Maid's Tragedy* (Beaumont and Fletcher, *ca.* 1611), *The White Devil* (1612), or *The Duchess of Malfi* (John Webster, *ca.* 1613). *The Revenger's Tragedy* (Cyril Tourneur, 1607), *The Changeling* (Thomas Middleton and William Rowley, *ca.* 1623), and *The Broken Heart* (*ca.* 1632), or *'Tis Pity She's a Whore* (John Ford, *ca.* 1626).

Corneille

Although English drama was virtually moribund, for a variety of political and religious reasons, during the middle decades of the seventeenth century, the theater in France was very much alive. Between the appearance of Corneille's *Le Cid* in 1636 and Racine's retirement from the stage in 1677, drama in France experienced a blossoming in many ways comparable in vigor and artistic stature with that which had taken place in Elizabethan England. The form taken by this outburst of dramatic vitality, however, was peculiarly French, and very different from the course followed across the Channel.

French "classical" drama—as it is called—was, it is true, the product of very much the same elements and forces that had produced Elizabethan drama a half century earlier: the grafting of Greek and Roman dramatic traditions onto native stock. But during the sixteenth century, while the consolidation and development of English drama were being carried forward in giant steps by men like Thomas Kyd and Christopher Marlowe and, of course, Shakespeare, the French popular theater was largely stagnant, remaining comparatively primitive in its dramaturgy and

133

134   medieval in its tone. The result was that, when the merging of
traditions took place, the native component was relatively feeble,
and the subsequent fusion was weighted heavily toward the Classical influence and toward the "rules" that the French critics,
rightly or wrongly, attributed to Classical authorities.

As a consequence, French classical drama is very different from
Elizabethan and Jacobean drama, and for readers familiar only
with the English tradition, it presents some very real difficulties.
The most obvious and immediate obstacle is that of the language.
It is, for one thing, poetic drama, and a full response is possible
only where the reader has sufficient proficiency in the language
that he can sense and respond to the subtler nuances of meaning,
the suggestiveness of words, the careful manipulation of tone, that
are characteristic of poetry. Many readers will, of necessity, get
around this obstacle by relying on translations; but a translation,
no matter how good, will never possess exactly the same qualities
as the original. It may, however, be adequate, and in any case the
"language barrier" is not sufficient in itself to explain the strangeness the reader will probably feel in the presence of French classical drama. After all, countless literary works have been rendered
into English out of unfamiliar tongues and foreign traditions in
such a way as to be perfectly accessible to the modern reader.
Witness the Greek tragedies, which can provide powerful dramatic
experiences without the music and dancing that originally ac-
companied them. There exist perfectly competent poetic translations of many of the plays of Corneille and Racine; but the
unfamiliarity and the difficulty persist, because they lie at a more
basic level than that of language.

French classical plays, as a group, are simply based on assumptions about human nature and social values, about the conventions
and scope of the theatrical illusion, and about the nature of
tragedy, quite different from the assumptions that formed the
basis of the Elizabethan theater. Compared to the plays of Shakespeare, those of Corneille and Racine seem at first glance somewhat rarefied, overly refined, decorous almost to the point of
being effete. With their high degree of stylization, an apparent

simplicity in plot, and an almost complete absence of physical 135
stage action, they seem brittle and artificial after the violent Elizabethans—and we may often wonder whether anything really
"happens" in these plays at all. Certainly we must not expect to
find the extravagant, mercurial, sometimes grotesque characters
of Shakespeare. There are no Falstaffs here, no Hotspurs or
Ancient Pistols or Justice Shallows—to take only the *Henry IV*
plays. In a word, if we approach these French plays from the
vantage point of Shakespeare and the Elizabethans, we shall be
at a total loss; and yet in France, this classical drama is regarded
as a dramatic achievement second—if that—only to Shakespeare's.

There is in the whole field of drama no more striking example
than this of the fundamental requirement already stated: that
the ability to participate in the dramatic experience depends on
a common view on the part of audience and playwright as to the
nature of the significant reality that is the proper subject of drama
and as to the conventions by which that reality can be represented on the stage. Because French classical drama is the product of a unique cultural and national heritage, it is not easy for
those of us not part of that heritage to respond to it. But it is not
inaccessible; and the rewards of some effort to understand it are
worthwhile.

Although the plays and playwrights subsumed under the label
of French classical drama have much in common, in terms of
both style and point of view, there are still significant individual
differences. The names of Pierre Corneille (1606-1684) and
Jean Racine (1639-1699) are frequently linked, but largely because they are the only representatives of the tradition readily
available, and therefore familiar, in English translation. Such a
blurring of distinctions, however, not only is unfair to the unique
genius of each but can blind us to the truly revealing similarities
by suggesting that they are alike in every respect.

Of the two, Corneille is probably the less accessible for a
variety of reasons. Most of his plays give the impression of being
rather dry and academic, offering rudimentary character develop-

ment and enlivened only by modest flights of rhetoric, of interest primarily to scholars. Only *Le Cid* (1636), an early play that established Corneille's reputation as a major playwright—albeit a controversial one—has proved to have much appeal to modern readers. This preference is perhaps unfair, but the reasons for it are perfectly apparent. *Le Cid* has all the familiar elements of melodrama: exalted passions, suspense, duels of honor, the ambush and defeat of superior forces by an extravagantly idealized hero, and of course the final union—at least implied—between him and an equally idealized heroine. This is the stuff of film "spectaculars," and indeed the story has received cinematic treatment. But the reader coming to the play with expectations based on the movie will inevitably be disappointed. The first thing that will strike him is that the language is not of a kind usually favored by Hollywood. It is poetic, in a stiff and formal way; but, far from possessing the richness and suggestiveness of Shakespeare's highly figurative style, Corneille's is deceptively simple, lucid, even stark, and especially in translation appears very flat and stilted indeed.

Then there is the lack of action; for, while the story is filled with melodramatic violence, it is largely only described, the events themselves taking place off stage. And the characters, in contrast to the complex and "rounded" characterizations so much admired in later criticism, seem one-dimensional sometimes to the point of simple-mindedness, often appearing obsessed by one or at most two clearly defined drives or ideals or emotions, to the exclusion of all else. Indeed, the area of human experience with which the play is concerned seems in itself strangely limited. The values appealed to, the motivations for the action, in a word the sources of the conflict that provide the basic fabric of any play, all appear so rigidly circumscribed in scope as to seem grotesquely out of proportion to the blood and passion they evoke.

The hypersensitive code of honor, so important to the characters in *Le Cid,* evolved partly out of the realities of medieval court life and partly out of the fictions of the chivalric romance, and seems to modern eyes unrealistic, trivial, and more than a little artificial. Indeed, the whole atmosphere of this play, where questions of honor are constantly at the dramatic center, can best be described as artificial.

As we have seen, the conflict in earlier tragedy, in that of the Greeks, in Marlowe's *Dr. Faustus,* for instance, and to an extent in Shakespeare's, was between man and the universe—or at least some kind of superhuman and cosmic forces that limit and baffle man and enshroud his fate in mystery. It is, in other words, the confrontation of man by something more than human. But in *Le Cid,* and in most of Corneille's plays, the conflict lies between two essentially "man-made" or at least man-centered forces: his passion and his sense of honor.

At least at first such a theme, especially when it is treated in play after play, seems disastrously narrow and even irrelevant; and much of the talk about honor may appear mere rhetorical bombast to swell a scene and assault our ear with "high-astounding" noise. Certainly the conflict is essentially social—that is, is concerned with man in his relationships with other men and with purely human institutions and codes. Consequently, it is possible that such drama will have meaning only to a society where these specific values and codes of behavior seem important, and that to the modern reader the mystery of the superhuman universe will appear reduced to the level of rarefied, hypersensitive, and therefore almost meaningless concepts of honor.

But in fact these ideas are not irrelevant, nor do we have to accept the supreme authority of honor per se for the plays to have meaning. In *Le Cid* in particular, and French classical drama in general, the conflict is not only between love and honor but between the human and the ideal; and the tragedy lies in the difficulty or even impossibility of living up to the ideal. The concern, in other words, is not with a *specific* ideal (such as honor), so much as with the general incompatibility of human nature and human existence with *any* rigid or absolute pattern of perfection, whether self-created or imposed by society.

Le Cid, for example, is constructed so as to represent its characters caught in a series of dilemmas growing out of conflicting and mutually exclusive demands or obligations or desires. The whole concept of duty and obligation is, of course, based on some notion of ideal behavior, and an ideal is almost inevitably an abstraction. Man, however, is not an abstraction but a thing of flesh and blood, capable perhaps of *conceiving* of an abstract ideal—of honor or of perfect love—without necessarily being able to fulfill that ideal in actual performance. And this fact, for the French classical playwrights, is a principal source of the tragic paradox.

Corneille is not, as some critics seem to assume, belittling extreme sensitivity to honor, nor criticizing man's capacity for abstractions, his ability to dream up impossible ideals for himself. The playwright seems rather to respect both the unrealistic ideals and the human passions that would burst the bonds of duty. He is simply observing, dramatically, this disruptive and often destructive ambivalence in man's nature, which has, in one way or another, been the subject of tragedy from the beginning. If there is also a note of regret, it is mitigated by the awareness that in this struggle lies the glory, as well as the tragedy, of man's existence.

In *Le Cid,* as in most French classical tragedies, the conflict or tension between the ideal and the real—or possible—is put in terms of the irreconcilable pulls of reason and emotion. The cultural and intellectual climate of seventeenth-century France encouraged this particular kind of antithesis. Much philosophical attention was being given to questions of man's rational powers, as well as to their limitations; and on the whole there was probably a greater faith in reason than we have today. Certainly reasonableness and common sense were taken as self-evident and absolute ideals in themselves. And other ideals of human behavior, such as the concept of honor and the concomitant notions of duty and loyalty to country, parents, friends, and the like, were arrived at, it was assumed, by the exercise of reason and realized by the exercise of will.

The characters in plays such as *Le Cid* are, above all, rational men and women. They are, for the most part, perfectly aware of all the aspects of the dilemmas in which they find themselves; and they try, however unsuccessfully, to follow the dictates of duty and reason. This explains in part why they appear rather cold and decorous as human beings and why their language tends to be simple, formal, and, as poetry, relatively unimaginative, or at least prosaic. Decorum, following the "rules," in social behavior, as well as lucidity and directness in communication, are rationally accessible ideals to which the age aspired, and they are embodied in its dramatic characters. But while the characters know the ideal and try to force themselves into its mold, they come up against a harsh fact: that either there are two ideals that cannot be fulfilled at the same time or there is something they passionately want, as human beings, that does not fit with *any* rational ideal. In either case, reason alone is not adequate to resolve the dilemma. The situation is one characteristic of tragedy: A specific and willful choice must be made, often a more clear-cut choice than is usual in "real life." And whichever path is taken, whichever horn of the dilemma is elected, it is only at terrible cost. If the course dictated by duty and reason is chosen, it is at the sacrifice of something passionately desired, usually the object of love. By the same token, the path of unreason and passion can be taken only at the price of something as dear as life itself—the capacity to live up to a rational ideal.

A brief outline of the plot of *Le Cid* will illustrate the way in which Corneille sets up a pattern of such dilemmas—their progressively increasing intensity providing the principal movement of the play.

The situation at the beginning of the play promises that duty and passion will not only be in complete accord but will in fact reinforce one another. Chimène and Roderick are in love and, what is more important in terms of the conventions of the age, their fathers, nobles in the court of Castile, approve the match. The opening scene emphasizes Chimène's great good fortune—although she does not quite trust in it—at being able to follow her duty to her father and her own impulse at the same time.

The second scene introduces a kind of subplot that has disturbed many critics of the play, since it seems to have little to do with the main line of the action. At first, however, it appears that we are being presented with the fly in the ointment—the third point in a conventional romantic triangle. The Infanta, or princess, of Castile is also in love with Roderick. However, since she never reveals the fact to anyone except her confidante, her passion has no effect whatever on either the course or the outcome of the play. And yet the scenes in which the Infanta discusses her hopeless love appear at regular intervals up to the very end. Their function, however, is not to further the action but to keep before us, in clear focus, both the values in terms of which we are to judge the principal characters and the two points of the dilemma in which they find themselves, honor and love.

The problem for the Infanta is that, while she desperately loves Roderick, both the laws of friendship (to Chimène) and her sense of duty (to her position as princess) are for her effective barriers to fulfillment. "So well do I remember [my duty]" she tells her confidante, "that I/Would kill myself ere I would stoop to be/ False to my station."[1] She has, in fact, actively encouraged the romance between Chimène and Roderick in order to remove temptation: "Till then, my anguish is beyond conception;/ For, till he weds, I cannot choose but love him. . . . I feel my soul divided: though my will/ Is strong, my breast is all aflame. . . . My honor and my love are both/ So dear to me that I shall die if either/ Of them surrenders or if either conquers" (I.ii). There could not be a more explicit statement of the kind of dilemma, or the torments, that the two principal lovers will have to face.

The mood of joyful optimism with which the play opens is quickly dispelled when, in the third scene, there is a falling out between the two fathers, characteristically over a question of honor. Don Diegue, Roderick's father, has been named mentor to the young prince of Castile in recognition of his former military exploits. The Count de Gormas, Chimène's father, is now what

---

[1] *Le Cid,* in *The Chief Plays of Corneille,* trans. Lacy Lockert (Princeton: Princeton University Press, 1957), Act. I, Scene ii. All quotations from Corneille are from this translation.

Don Diegue had been, chief of the king's warriors, and takes his
failure to be given the appointment as tutor as a slur on his serv-
ices and on his honor. In his bitterness, he strikes and then dis-
arms Don Diegue, who is too feeble with age to resist the outrage.

Don Diegue, on his part, sees the insult as an insupportable blot
on *his* honor. Unrevenged, he feels he cannot accept the dignity
given him by the king nor ever hold up his head again; but he is
too old to set matters right himself. In desperation, he begs his
son, Roderick, to free the family name from this cloud: "So great
an outrage/ 'Tis fatal to the honor of us both./ A blow in the
face! . . . Nothing but blood atoneth for a blow. . . . Show that
thou art thy father's worthy son" (I.iii).

Both father and son are quite aware that the blood must be
that of Chimène's father; and in a soliloquy at the end of Act I
Roderick contemplates the equally disastrous alternatives that
face him, considering the possibility of escape through death:

> Nay, better die at once! To her
> I love, I owe no less than to my sire.
> To avenge him will incur for me her ire;
> To avenge him not will her contempt incur.
> I must behave as though I do not love her
> Or be unworthy of her.

In other words, not only would a failure to avenge his father be
an act of disrespect to him but, in his own loss of honor, he would
become unworthy of Chimène's love—which he will also lose if
he *does* kill her father. But escaping the dilemma by suicide would
also be dishonorable:

> What! die, and leave redress ungained?
> Desire an ignominious death to die?
> Endure that Spain should recollect that I
> Have ill the honor of my house maintained?
>
>   *   *   *
>
> Let me henceforth shun thoughts so base and low.

Thus, at the end of Act I, we have established the impossible
alternatives that in one way or another will haunt Roderick, and
the other characters, throughout the play. At this point, the only

way out seems to be for Chimène's father to apologize publicly for his insult; but this would itself, he feels, involve a loss of honor that he cannot face.

When Roderick and the Count leave to fight their duel of honor offstage, Chimène restates in her own terms the central dilemma:

> If he obeyed me not, what crowning pain!
> And if he did obey me, what would men
> Say of him! Being born his father's son,
> Is he, forsooth, to suffer such an outrage?
> Whether he yields or does not to the love
> Which binds him to me, I must either be
> Ashamed of his excessive pliancy
> Or crushed by his refusal, however just.

Since only one man, her father or her lover, can emerge alive from the duel, her anguish is without hope. When Roderick returns victorious, Chimène immediately appeals to the king to avenge her father's death, which she, as a woman, cannot do for herself. But, as she says: "I ask his head and fear to gain my prayer" (III.i). She is now roughly in the situation in which Roderick had found himself before:

> One half my heart sends to the grave the other
> And by that fatal blow makes me avenge
> That which I lost on that which yet is left me!
>
>   *   *   *
>
> But in this dreadful war of wrath and love,
> Although my heart is torn, my will is firm;
> And whatsoever hold my love hath on me,
> I shall not hesitate to do my duty.
> I walk unfalteringly the path of honor.
> Roderick is very dear to me. I grieve
> For him; my heart is with him; but despite
> Its struggles, I forget not that I am
> My father's daughter and that he is dead. (III.i.)

And ironically, as she points out, it is Roderick's example that has given her the strength of will to follow the hard path of duty rather than the softer one of love:

Concepts of Reality in the Great Periods of Drama

Howe'er in thy behalf our love pleads with me,
My strength of soul must be no less than thine.
In wronging me thou provedst thyself worthy
Of me. By *thy* death I must prove myself
Worthy of thee.

The two young lovers are placed in this incongruous situation
not only because their strong concept of duty is incompatible with
their passion, but because to violate their ideal of honor would
make either one unworthy of their high ideal of love. In other
words the conflict is two-fold: between reason and emotion on
the one hand, and between two essentially rational ideals on the
other.

It is not necessary to quote in detail all the soul-searching and
tormented discussion that these two go through in explaining all
the ramifications of their predicament to themselves and to each
other. The problem is constantly changing, and yet always the
same. Roderick offers to satisfy Chimène's need to avenge her
father by giving himself up to her as his executioner; but she
points out that there is no honor in killing a man who will not
defend himself, and in any case, "My father and my honor shall
owe nothing/ To promptings of thy love or thy despair" (III.i).

Roderick is called away from his love-and-honor struggle to
lead a group of knights who ambush and defeat a superior force
of invading Moors. Chimène, characteristically, is torn between
fear for her lover's life and a fear that a glorious death would
cheat her of her revenge.

I ask his death, but not a glorious death,
Not one so splendid that it would exalt him. (IV.ii)

And yet, of course, this is at least partly sheer rationalization.
Roderick, on his part, is probably a little more honest with himself when he says that he had again considered a possible "escape"
by permitting the Moors to kill him, but that his sense of honor
prevented him from such a betrayal of his country and of his own
dignity.

Roderick returns from battle to be greeted as savior of his
country and its chief warrior; but Chimène interrupts the king's

praises to demand justice in her father's name. She finally forces the king to permit her to follow an old tradition and allow her, with the court's sanction, to name a "defender" to fight her cause in a duel with Roderick. The king reluctantly agrees, but only on condition that Chimène marry the victor and hence free him of her irritating demands. Once again, the girl finds herself in a hopeless situation, where she must marry either "him I detest or him whose death I sought!/ The slayer of my father or of Roderick!"—and in a frenzy of despair she denounces both vengeance and love, as the source of nothing but turmoil and anguish.

When Chimène's "defender" appears, her true feelings break out in her wail of heartbreak at her imagined loss. It turns out, however, that he has come, at Roderick's command, to lay his sword at her feet as symbol of his defeat by her lover. Chimène still tries to brave it out, and to insist that the king respect her honor and her father's memory by not forcing her to marry his murderer. But things have gone too far, and she is forced, in violation not of her will but of her sense of duty, to accept the compromise insisted on by the king: She will marry Roderick in a year's time.

And the conclusion *is* a compromise. Chimène's last words are to remind the king that in obeying him she must live with "eternal reproach" for having betrayed her father; and to his offer of a year's grace she has nothing further to say. In a sense, then, the central conflict between love and a desire to be true to an absolute ideal of human behavior is left partially unresolved or, if it is resolved, only arbitrarily so, by a fiat from outside. Perhaps Corneille is suggesting that ultimately this is the only possible adjustment of goals or values that are inherently incompatible.

Le Cid is not tragedy, at least in the usual sense, although it does not actually violate Aristotelian precepts. We might call it a tragicomedy, if we can ignore that term's pejorative overtones. The ending is neither facile nor unconvincingly "happy," since there is no real resolution, and Chimène's happiness is, for her, tainted. And certainly the play could not be passed off as melodrama. The physical action is largely peripheral to the real action,

the real conflict, which lies in the nature and souls of the characters.

A reality that is intentionally of such narrow scope seems, to modern eyes, so restricted as to render the characters and situations dehumanized and flat. But as in so many cases, the full effect is possibly achieved only on the stage. Just as the concern of the play, and its effect, grow out of the tension between abstractions and physical or emotional realities, so the characters on the stage represent a curious fusion of real men and women—that is, the actors—and abstractions—the way in which they talk and act and the ideals they enunciate. The dichotomy, and hence the sense of strain, is real and dramatic; and while both the reality being considered and the technique being employed severely restrict the range of dramatic effects that can be obtained, the very narrowness of Corneille's scope gives his plays an intensity that belies their apparent artificiality.

Racine

Racine, writing at roughly the same time as Corneille and for a similar audience, not unnaturally shares some of his concerns and assumptions. He too desired to emulate the ancients and to adapt their principles and rules to the French stage. And in most of his plays the dramatic structure and tension derive from the opposition of an ideal of abstract duty and some irrational drive or desire, usually love. But the violence of the conflict and our awareness of it are, if possible, even more intense.

Corneille, in *Le Cid,* can admit at least the possibility of compromise. Roderick, if not Chimène, is able to achieve both love and duty without sacrificing either, although he is, as an essentially rational being, willing to *risk* love as the lesser obligation. Racine, on the other hand, although his plays are generally less melodramatic in their plots than *Le Cid,* creates an even greater dramatic tension by emphasizing the wholly irreconcilable and mutually exclusive nature of rationally derived ideals of duty and honor—subsumed under the concept of "gloire"—and violent and uncontrollable human passions.

This sense of absolute and uncompromisable opposition is nowhere more apparent than in Racine's best-known play, *Phaedra* (1677). The plot is taken virtually in its entirety from the *Hippolytus* of Euripides; but Racine has made it, thematically and dramatically, entirely his own.

The strong feeling of violence, both potential and actual, that pervades this play is due in large part to the fact that Racine places in opposition ideals of duty and passions that are, even within their respective spheres, extremes. But before introducing the central conflict, he offers a norm or standard by which those extremes may be judged.

The play begins with the appearance of Hippolytus, a youth renowned for his virtue and integrity. A great hunter and athlete, he has prided himself that he has never succumbed to the softer emotions of love. In this scene, however, he reveals to his tutor (and servant) that he is so far human as to have fallen in love with the beautiful young princess, Aricia. He has never professed his love; indeed, he scarcely acknowledges it to himself, for there is an insuperable barrier to its fulfillment. Aricia's brothers had rebelled against King Theseus, Hippolytus' father; and although the brothers are dead, the king

> Holds her in reprobation, and forbids her
> Ever to marry: of a guilty stem
> He fears a shoot, and wishes to entomb
> With her the memory of her brothers' name.[1]

Faced with his father's absolute prohibition, Hippolytus has determined to leave home and forget in the pursuit of glorious deeds his hopeless and impossible love. His tutor, with a disregard for the ideals of honor and filial duty characteristic of servants in French classical drama, urges Hippolytus to follow his impulses:

[1] *Phaedra*, in *Jean Racine: Five Plays*, trans. Kenneth Muir (New York: Hill & Wang, Inc., 1960), Act I, Scene i. All quotations from Racine are from this translation.

> If your hour is come,
> My Lord, heaven cares not for our reasons.

* * *

> If it is sweet, why should you not dare taste it?
> Why will you trust a shy or sullen scruple?

But the youth refuses to be dissuaded from his sense of duty by facile arguments and is adamant in his determination to flee from a forbidden passion. This, for Racine, obviously represents an ideal pattern of rational behavior. Hippolytus, as a human being, cannot control his emotions, but as a man with a keen sense of duty, he *can* control his actions.

This scene is followed immediately by a parallel episode between Phaedra and her nurse, in which she, like Hippolytus, confesses a secret passion. It is not, however, like his an honest and normal love; for it is adulterous, in that she is married to Theseus, and incestuous, in that its object is her own stepson, Hippolytus. Indeed, it is not love at all, but a wild infatuation bordering on madness:

> I felt my body freeze and burn; I knew
> The terrible fires of Venus, the tortures fated
> To one whom she pursues. (I.iii)

"I sought for my lost reason," she continues, in religious observance, "Weak remedies of love incurable!"

Although she is unable to control her passion, Phaedra is as much aware as Hippolytus of her falling off from an ideal and, like him, seeks escape:

> I have a just abhorrence of my crime;
> I hate my life, abominate my lust;
> Longing by death to rescue my good name.

At this desperate juncture a messenger arrives with the news that Theseus is dead. The coincidental timing of this revelation is unquestionably improbable, but Racine is concerned not with the "realism" of the action but with the new set of conditions this creates for his characters. The nurse persuades Phaedra that now her "love becomes a usual love" and that she has everything to live for. Strictly speaking, this is a rationalization, since Theseus' death does not of itself alter either the nature of her love or her guilt; but Phaedra is all too anxious to be drawn by the easy logic of the nurse.

The passing of Theseus does, however, remove the purely legal prohibition against Aricia's marrying, as Hippolytus quickly realizes. Act II contains two scenes exactly paralleling those in Act I. In the first, Hippolytus meets with Aricia to discuss his plans for dividing his father's kingdom with her and Phaedra. His discussion, at first, is completely self-controlled and rational, but gradually his feelings get the better of him. As he terms it: "Reason yields to violence," although his only violence is a halting confession that he is "now enslaved under the common law" and is in love. Aricia obviously reciprocates; but the meeting is interrupted by a request from Phaedra that Hippolytus come to her. He goes, and in a brilliantly constructed speech beginning with the words "I pine and burn for Theseus," Phaedra gradually substitutes the image of Hippolytus for that of Theseus as the object of her "burning"; and bit by bit the true meaning of her words dawns on the horrified youth. Even in the midst of open avowal the distraught woman tries to cling to her honor by acknowledging her guilt:

> I love; but do not think that I condone it,
> Or think it innocent; nor that I ever
> With base complaisance added to the poison
> Of my mad passion. . . . I abhor myself. . . . (II.v)

Her self-abhorrence is not sufficient, however, to keep her passion under control; and when Hippolytus' only response is to remind her that "Theseus is my father,/ And you his wife," all she has gained, as she knew it would be, is shame and frustration.

Act III traces the complete moral dissolution of Phaedra under the force of her passion. Having, as she says, "crossed the bounds of rigid modesty," there is no turning back, and she gives free reign to her infatuation. When the nurse suggests that she seek peace in the distractions of affairs of state, she replies:

I reign? To place the State
Under my law, when reason reigns no longer
Over myself; when I have abdicated
From the empire of my senses. (III.i)

And when the nurse then urges her to take flight: "All your coun-
sels now/ Are out of season. Serve my passion, Oenone,/ And
not my reason." Indeed, she begs the nurse to go and plead with
Hippolytus, hoping she can soften his distaste for her advances.

But when Oenone returns, it is with news that drastically alters
the situation. Theseus is not dead, but has landed and is at that
moment approaching his home and his queen. In a spasm of fear
and shame, Phaedra once more determines to die; but the nurse
protests that suicide would be a confession of guilt and that to die
dishonored is the worst thing that could happen to her. To clear
her name, she urges Phaedra to turn the tables on Hippolytus,
who she supposes will accuse her to Theseus, and to claim that
he has tried to seduce his stepmother:

But even if
His guiltless blood is spilt, your threatened honor
Is yet too valuable to be exposed.
Whatever it demands, you must submit,
Madam. And to save your threatened honor
All must be sacrificed, including virtue. (III.iii)

Phaedra's will power and moral sense have by now so far disin-
tegrated that she fails to see the speciousness of Oenone's argument: that the "honor" she would gain is only reputation and
appearance; that honor purchased with dishonor is inherently
sick. But her judgment has been consumed by her passion: "Do
what you will,/ I resign myself to you. In my disorder,/ I can do
nothing for myself."

When Theseus appears, Phaedra only makes some vague allusions to a dreadful occurrence during his absence and leaves her
puzzled husband to query Hippolytus. But he is too honorable,
in the true sense of the word, to reveal his stepmother's shame
and only begs his father to allow him to leave home and by noble
deeds abroad, "prove to all the world/ I was your son."

French Classical Drama

Theseus is troubled by his apparently cold reception at home
and is ripe for the nurse's denunciation of his son at the beginning
of Act IV. And his reaction is instantaneous. It is as though passion breeds passion, and irrationality spreads like a virulent
plague. Without questioning the nurse's tale or confronting either
of the principals, Theseus flies into a fury. When Hippolytus
enters, he has no chance to defend himself from the denunciations
of his father, who takes advantage of a promise from the god
Neptune to grant him one wish and calls down a curse of utter
destruction on his son. When Theseus finally gives Hippolytus a
chance to speak, the latter does not defend himself with counter
accusations, but tries to point out, in a cool and rational argument,
how improbable the nurse's story must appear to a reasonable
judgment and that, far from being infatuated with Phaedra, his
heart belongs wholly to Aricia. But Theseus' judgment is no
longer reasonable; the very calmness with which his son defends
himself infuriates him, and every argument serves to feed his
rage.

Having ordered his son out of both home and country, Theseus
does talk with Phaedra, who makes a feeble attempt, not to con-
fess her guilt, but to soften her husband's wrath at his son. But
when she hears Hippolytus' defense, that he was in fact in love
with Aricia, her passion returns redoubled, transformed from the
madness of lust to a madness of jealousy and hate:

> O pain I never knew before!
> To what new torment am I now reserved!
> All I have suffered, all my frenzied fears,
> My passion's fury and its fierce remorse,
> The unbearable insult of his cruel repulse,
> Shadowed but feebly what I now endure. (IV.vi)

Not only must Hippolytus suffer, but Aricia:

> I cannot bear
> A joy which is an outrage to me. Oenone,
> Take pity on my jealous rage. That girl
> Must be destroyed; the anger of my husband

This is the low point in Phaedra's moral breakdown, where the violence of her passions has swept away the last vestige of rationality or self-control. But suddenly something clicks in her maddened mind, some dim memory of what she once was, and she stops abruptly in the midst of her wild outburst: "But what am I doing?/ Where has my reason fled?" A realization of what she has done, and what she wants to do, horrifies her newly awakened soul, and she determines once again to find escape in death. Oenone tries to stop her with her old argument that it is foolish to be too strict in moral matters: "Frailty is but too natural to us all./ You are a mortal—bow to mortal's lot." But Phaedra is now too keenly aware of the consequences of such facile reasoning, and turns on the nurse: "It was your pleading/ Made me forget my duty," and banishes her from her presence with a curse.

In Act V we return to sanity and the healthy love of Hippolytus and Aricia. In a series of lovely speeches, characterized by warmth moderated by self-control, and devotion combined with a sure sense of honor, the young people pledge their mutual faiths. They will be married in a temple outside the gates of the city, and Aricia will joyfully share Hippolytus' life of exile.

But the beast of passion has broken the bonds of control and cannot be so easily called to heel. Although Phaedra has regained her lost reason and Theseus has second thoughts about his rash curse, what has been done cannot be undone. The reasonable and honorable love of Aricia and Hippolytus, at the very moment of its fulfillment, is brutally destroyed by a tangible symbol of the irrationality and animal-like passion that Phaedra, and to a lesser extent Theseus, have loosed into the world. A monstrous beast from the sea, called up by Theseus' curse, hurls itself at Hippolytus' chariot as he leaves the city; and dragged by his maddened horses, he arrives, a mass of broken and bloody flesh, at the feet of Aricia.

After such violence, the play ends rather restrainedly. Phaedra, having recovered her self-control, sadly confesses her guilt to her husband; and Theseus, realizing the implications regarding *his* guilt, mournfully expresses the hope that he may "expiate [his] madness" by henceforth treating Aricia as his daughter.

The power of *Phaedra,* as has been suggested, lies in great part in the absolute irreconcilability of two absolute demands, of reason and duty and honor on the one hand, and of ungovernable passion on the other. The violence of the play lies not so much in the *expression* of passion as in the sense of the intensity of the struggle between these demands—of passion suppressed by duty and reason, and of rationality overwhelmed and itself suppressed by man's passionate nature. But for the play to have meaning, the validity and strength of the ideal of reason and duty must be taken for granted. It is this reality that Racine assumes as "given" among his audience; and it is this reality that lies at the heart of the play.

To a large degree, the genius of Racine lies in the fact that the tone, the language, the movement of his plays are so organically related to—and reflect—his subject matter. Paradoxically, the intensity of feeling and violence of passion felt in his plays derives in part from an even more rigid observance of the rules of unity, decorum, and restraint than is true of Corneille. This phenomenon raises some interesting questions about the effectiveness and even validity of an art that is forced to conform to arbitrary restrictions. Our age is one in which, at least in theory, we value "freedom," in art as in social mores and political practices. And even if we accept as axiomatic the principle that art, by its very nature, presupposes rules of some sort, we might well expect rules that are very rigid and narrow, that limit style, subject matter, propriety, even diction and language, to be a strait jacket and produce something essentially lifeless and unreal. On the other hand, we also know that while certain substances may burn harmlessly in the open air, put into a container they will explode—and, up to a point, the more rigid the container the more violent the explosion.

It is to a great extent the very restraints that Racine accepts, the understatement he is forced to practice, the violence that is only *implied,* that give his plays their tremendous vitality and impact. If the action in Racine's plays seems greater than in Corneille's, it is largely an illusion created by this heightened, at times almost unbearable, tension. The characters are put—or put themselves—in situations of incredible pressures, and yet the literary surface is always one of formality, decorum, extreme stylization. But the graceful, logical rhythms of the language, the slow, balanced pace, only serve to intensify our awareness of barely suppressed violence. The strain between the extremes of passion, which we know boil inside, and the rigidly controlled mask that must, by convention, be kept on, creates an explosive tension that is highly dramatic. This technique is effective, however, not only because it is a skillfully handled dramatic device but because it reflects an ideal of human behavior, of self-control and decorum, that was part of the cultural heritage the audience would have brought to the play, and hence part of the reality they would have found in it.

Sometimes, in Racine's plays as in real life, the internal pressure becomes too great, and the rigid container of self-control cracks under the strain. This happens in *Phaedra;* and the language and its rhythms reflect, to an extent, the uncontrolled disorder of the soul. This is most evident in some of the conversations between Phaedra or Theseus and Hippolytus, who embodies, without lapse, the ideal of restraint and decorum.

There are plays, however, in which the impending or potential explosion never comes, where the spirit represented by Hippolytus reigns supreme. And in such plays the dramatic tension can be even more intense than in *Phaedra,* simply because the rigidly controlled inner pressures never *do* find release. A somewhat earlier play, *Berenice* (1670), is in this sense one of the finest examples of Racine's techniques and genius.

At the simplest level, *Berenice* is based on the well-worn situation of the romantic triangle; but the relevance of this situation to either plot or theme is peripheral, since at the end the triangle is as unresolved as at the beginning. Indeed, in a sense this is a play in which absolutely nothing happens. In the course of the action no loves are fulfilled, no unexpected recognitions take place, no deaths occur. All three of the major characters are royalty and as such are keenly aware of the ideals of duty and honor and self-control that they are expected to exemplify, and in the end they are all true to them. The only thing that "happens" is that, for each of them, these ideals are put to a supreme test; and what they learn is not the *theory* of stern idealism but the painful reality.

At the beginning of the play, Titus, at the death of his father Vespasian, has just become Emperor of Rome. He has long been in love with Berenice, Queen of Palestine, who is at the time in Rome, as is Antiochus, King of Comagena, who has been for some years secretly devoted to Berenice. As the play opens, it is expected that Titus will at any moment ask Berenice to become his Empress. Antiochus, as a former comrade-in-arms of Titus, has too much loyalty to his old friend to interfere in his romance; and when he realizes that Berenice returns the Emperor's passion, he determines to leave Rome and his hopeless love. Unknown to him and Berenice, however, an obstacle to Titus' marriage has arisen. There is an unwritten law in Rome that a "foreigner," as Berenice is, cannot become Empress, and Titus is forced to come face to face, as he has not before, with the fact that his position as Emperor involves an uncompromisable responsibility to the traditions of his country and the will of his people. Broken-hearted, he tries, rather inadequately, to explain his situation to Berenice; but she is so full of the joy of a love she imagines is about to be fulfilled that she does not understand his meaning. In desperation, Titus asks Antiochus, as an office of friendship, to tell Berenice the truth. Torn between pity for her and hopes for his own cause, he does so; but she refuses to believe him and, accusing him of trying to come between her and Titus, orders him never to see her again. Berenice rushes off to confront

ing his absolute responsibilities to Rome. As he tells her:

> . . . recognize
> The voice of duty. It is time for it.
> Compel your love to silence: with an eye
> Enlightened both by honor and by reason
> Look on my duty in its sternest guise. (IV. v.)

His self-assurance is shaken by the force of her passion; and
when she leaves, threatening suicide, he is almost crushed by the
dilemma:

> I hate myself. Not even Nero pushed
> His cruelty so far. I'll not endure
> That Berenice should die. Come. Let Rome say
> What she would say.

>   *   *   *

>   Rome! Berenice!
> Unfortunate Prince! Why am I Emperor?
> Why do I love? (IV. vi)

At this point Antiochus enters to plead with him to go to Berenice
and save her life; but at the same moment a messenger comes
to ask the Emperor's presence at the Senate. After only a moment's hesitation, Titus goes to the Senate.

At the beginning of the last act, Antiochus receives word that
Berenice, having learned of Titus' decision to go to the Senate
rather than come to her, is on the point of leaving Rome in anger
rather than despair. But his momentary flush of hope is quickly
extinguished by the appearance of Titus, on his way to try once
more to convince Berenice of his love.

In this last meeting, Titus appears as a man all but destroyed
by inner turmoil, but clinging desperately to the one solid ideal of
honor. As he had earlier been unthinking and careless of the
future in his love, so, he confesses, had he assumed the course of
duty would be easier and more clearly defined than it proved.
Now, he says,

> I myself can hardly recollect
> If I am Emperor, or even Roman.
> I've come to you not knowing my intent,
> Brought by my love; and came perhaps to seek
> Myself, and know myself. (V.vi)

What he has learned is that in spite of his great love—indeed, because of it—he cannot betray himself, because the honor of that self is intimately tied to his responsibilities as Emperor:

> To whatever straits
> You have reduced me, my unpitying honor
> Pursues me every moment. It presents
> The Empire ceaselessly to my dazed soul
> As incompatible with our marriage still;
> . . . I ought to wed you
> Now less than ever; and still less [should I] tell you
> That I am ready to forsake the Empire
> To follow you, contented with my chains,
> To sigh with you at the world's end. For you
> Yourself would blush at my base conduct then.

His love is too great to taint it with dishonor. But if, he goes on, she persists in her threats to destroy herself, he can be true to both his love and his sense of honor only by following her in death.

Before the Queen can answer, Antiochus enters to make a last pledge of love to his two friends before he too commits suicide.

> For the last time I've communed with my self;
> I've made a last proof of my courage now;
> My senses are restored. I never felt
> More in love. I shall need other efforts
> To break so many knots; only by death
> Can I destroy them; so I hasten to it. (V.vii)

In other words, since he cannot stifle a love that can no longer be honorable, he will destroy it in the only way he can, with his life.

Moved by such expressions of a sense of honor, and convinced at last of Titus' undying devotion, Berenice realizes that her insistence on her own private love is something less than worthy.

> I wish, at this tragic time, by a last effort
> To crown the rest. I shall go on living now.
> I shall obey your absolute commands.
> Farewell, my lord. Reign, I shall not see you more.

And turning to Antiochus:

> I cannot leave the one I love, to go
> Far from Rome, to listen to other vows.
> Live also: make, my lord, a generous effort
> To rule your conduct by Titus and by me.
> I love him, and I flee him.

As the play ends, the three sadly go their separate ways, worthy of each others' loves only by setting their own loves second to their ideals of honor and duty.

It is impossible to communicate the effect of *Berenice* in a barren summary of the plot. It is true that in a real sense it is a static play. It is an exemplification of the ideals of honor, loyalty, and decorum, and its movement lies simply in the gradual and painful exposure, in a series of taut but subdued scenes, of exactly what is implied in those ideals. But once again, the tension between the deep and powerful emotions and the self-control that honor imposes is highly effective dramatically. *Berenice,* perhaps better than any other play, demonstrates that within its self-imposed limits of style and subject matter—and in fact because of them—French classical drama, although it makes special demands on its audiences, also can give very special rewards.

Molière

Although the modern reader generally has more trouble coming to terms with the tragedy and heroic tragicomedy of French classical drama than with its comedy, no discussion of the period would be complete without some consideration of the work of Jean Poquelin, better known as Molière (1622-1673).

Obviously we would not expect to find the same elements in

his plays as in the tragedies just considered, because he was writing comedy. At the same time, Molière was roughly a contemporary of Corneille and Racine, and while he owed much more to the medieval tradition—specifically to its farce—than did the other two, he was by no means immune from the same pressures for observing the "rules" of the ancients, and the dramatic models for his comedies were as much Roman as medieval. But because he was writing comedy, Molière was somewhat less restricted by the demands of formality and decorum in style, language, and subject matter. Or, to be more accurate, decorum was interpreted differently in the case of comedy. The class of the characters represented was not normally that of the nobility or aristocracy but the middle and lower classes. And since the merchant or the shopkeeper or the servant was not expected to comprehend the meaning of "gloire" or to value the ideals of decorum and honor, his language and behavior could be treated with far greater freedom. Violence of action, so carefully avoided in tragedy, at least on the stage, was permitted, and frequently took the form of "slapstick," or physical, humor. The similarities between Molière and his more dignified colleagues, then, does not lie in matters of style or language or character portrayal, but rather in the *kind* of reality with which they are centrally concerned.

Where Corneille and Racine had found the source of tragic tension in the disparity between the ideal and the actual, or humanly fallible, in man's behavior, Molière found in it the source of comedy. The difference, then, is not so much in the "facts" being considered as in the tone and treatment. French classical tragedy is "social" in the sense that the ideals of honor, duty, and self-control are in effect socially determined values. And Molière's is "social" comedy in that it exposes to our laughter the ridiculousness of a failure to live or act in accord with social norms. The difference is largely that the ideals implicit in French classical tragedy are *ideal*—perfection; and the failure to live up to them, or the high cost where they *are* lived up to, is the inevitable consequences of our being human. The ideal in Molière's comedy is more human, more attainable, for it is simply the ordinary "common-sense" behavior of intelligent and reasonable men and women. The failure in tragedy only reaffirms our common humanity; the failure in comedy often suggests a kind of sub-humanity—a falling off from even a charitable image of human nature. The dividing line is a narrow one, and in many of Molière's comedies it would take only a small shift in tone and treatment to render an object of laughter—a Harpagon or an Alceste —pathetic, if not actually tragic. However, the small shift is *not* made; and instead of being made to feel that falling short of the ideal is a regrettable but probably inescapable condition of man's existence, we are given a representation of life where the deviation from the norm appears grotesque, ridiculous, absurd—in a sense, deformed.

There is some danger, because of the titles of Molière's plays, that we may assume that he is simply ridiculing specific kinds of social deformity: miserliness, misanthropy, social pretensions, and so on. But the source of his comedy—that is, the point at which it touches us—is the much broader truth that unbalance, obsession, one-sidedness of any sort, not only distorts our vision in some basic way but makes us less than human, hence grotesque and ridiculous.

We do not need Molière to tell us that miserliness is a social and moral evil; and so his emphasis is not ethical. What he does in *The Miser* (1668) is to anatomize this particular aberration as a symptom of a more basic failure, the consequence of a set of values, or a view of life, that is so distorted as to have lost contact with reality; and it is represented as not so much wrong as self-defeating.

In the scene where Harpagon, the miser, is giving directions for the banquet to be given in honor of what he hopes is his bride-to-be, he instructs the cook to make sure that the stew is largely fat—since it is not only cheap but will effectively suppress his guests' appetites—and reminds the waiters not to serve wine until asked the third time, and then well mixed with water. A minor touch, to be sure, but one that is simply part of a consistent portrait of a man for whom money has become the only

French Classical Drama

160   relevant consideration in any situation. It is more important than
the esteem of his friends, or the respect and love of his own children. It is more important than a wife, or than love itself. Indeed,
it *is* his love: "Oh dear, my dear, darling money, my beloved."[1]
This is a man for whom the acquisition of gold and the avoidance
of its loss have become the only meaningful values. He is extravagantly suspicious of everyone around him—his servants, his
friends, his children, and even, in the wildly farcical scene at the
end of Act IV, of himself. Indeed, his obsessive avarice and fear
have so effectively removed Harpagon from the world of reality
that he is totally incapable of *doing* anything, except negatively—
keeping money from those who could use it. He cannot be a
friend, he cannot be a father to his children, he cannot be a husband; in fact, far from giving him strength and power, his passion
for money has rendered him completely impotent.

Instead of being a positive force in healthy and productive
relationships—as the equally wealthy Anselme is—Harpagon is
simply an inert barrier. His lust for money not only replaces normal human emotions in him but blocks their fulfillment in others.
His greed is an almost insuperable obstacle to the romantic hopes
of his son and daughter. Furthermore, his perversion of normal
human relations corrupts his whole household, and everyone in
it has to pretend, lie, be a hypocrite wherever he is concerned. As
Jacques, the cook, learns from his ill-fated attempt to be honest
with Harpagon: "So much for sincerity! It's a poor sort of trade.
From now on I've done with it. No more telling the truth" (p.
144). Not only the servants but his children, Cléante and Élise,
are forced to hide their feelings from their father; Valère has to
play a role and be a hypocrite to win Élise, and Cléante resorts
to all kinds of subterfuge to woo Marianne. But these others,
while *living* in Harpagon's distorted and unreal world, have their
feet in reality and can *use* appearances—and his obsession—to
achieve their own ends.

[1] *The Miser,* in *The Miser and Other Plays,* trans. John Wood (Balti-
more: Penquin Books, Inc., 1962), Act III. All quotations from the play
are from this translation.

Molière represents his miser as a man wholly divorced from reality, from normal human relations—impotent, deformed, and hence grotesque and laughable. But he is not merely subhuman, and therefore contemptible. While it is true that he has replaced all human love with a love of gold, this is a passion that in its intensity is very human. Money has indeed become his mistress, and when it is stolen his desolation is sincere: "My beloved, they've taken you away from me and now you are gone and I have lost my strength, my joy and my consolation. . . . I can't go on living without you" (p. 159). The very violence of his grief, while comic, at the same time verges on pathos.

Harpagon's failure lies not only in having replaced normal human values with purely financial ones, but in that as a human being he cannot be sufficiently *true* to those false values. To be an effective—a *perfect*—miser, Harpagon should be as cold and heartless as the gold he worships. Being human, he must love; but the object of his passion cannot return it. And it is to a great extent the futility, the frustration, the hysteria of that love that renders Harpagon impotent.

What we have here, in a sense, is an inversion of the typical pattern of French classical tragedy: a character who is dedicated to a kind of "anti-ideal," but who, in his humanity, cannot live up to it. We can see much the same pattern in *Tartuffe* (1669), where the clever, Machiavellian rogue of the title is coldly and efficiently exploiting the gullible Orgon for all he is worth, but is betrayed by his all-too-human passion for Orgon's wife. Tartuffe falls off from his ideal of "perfect" villainy, which involves a pose of contempt for all things of the flesh, just because he is *not* inhuman.

Molière, then, in a sense plays his game two ways at once. A character may deviate widely from the norm of healthy, reasonable behavior, and hence become deformed and ridiculous; but not absolutely. Because he is still a man, there is also a "failure" to be wholly nonhuman; and by bringing him back toward the norm Molière both keeps him within the scope of humanity and makes him doubly laughable.

French Classical Drama

Perhaps Molière's most subtle and complex play is *The Misanthrope* (1666). Here again he deals with the disparity between an ideal and deviations from it, but he complicates the situation by introducing the ideal of superhuman perfection that until now we have associated with tragedy. What we have is really an inversion of the situation in *The Miser* and *Tartuffe*. Just as Harpagon deviates from normal rational behavior in the direction of a non- and subhuman "ideal," which he is unable to realize, so the misanthrope, Alceste, is moving in the direction of a *super*human ideal. Alceste's problem is that he cannot accept what he considers the pretense, the hypocrisy, the dishonesty, demanded by a polished, highly artificial society. The representatives of this society at its worst, Oronte, Célimène, or the two Marquises, are indeed so caught up in their elaborate game of scandal, flattery, and self-display that they, to only a slightly lesser extent than Harpagon, have become wholly divorced from anything that might reasonably be called reality or from any normal unselfish human emotions. They are, in other words, grotesque and ridiculous. But Alceste too is rendered grotesque by his own loss of contact with reality and by the absoluteness with which he refuses to accept the ordinary and everyday compromises with strict truth that are requisites for reasonable human social intercourse. And Alceste, like Tartuffe, although he presumes to an impossible ideal of rationality and virtue, is humanly irrational in his passionate love for the embodiment of all that he hates most, Célimène.

In between the superhuman and the subhuman stands Philinte, the embodiment of the common-sense compromise, who sees the folly and hypocrisy of his society and yet can live with it without becoming *of* it. In a sense, however, nobody wins. Célimène and Oronte are only foolish; Philinte, as a compromiser, is almost too reasonable to be anything but colorless, or to gain anything more than a qualified admiration; and Alceste, the idealist, who *might* be the object of respect, by his very idealism betrays his common sense and makes himself ridiculous.

The play is a tour de force; and if it comes to no clear-cut judgments, it does not need to. Its purpose—and the same could be said of any of Molière's comedies—is not to delimit certain attitudes or forms of behavior as "good" or "bad," but to derive laughter from the prospect of the disparity between an ideal behavior (whether established by society or simply by common sense) and the way mortals, in their frailty, actually *will* behave regardless of the ideal before them.

SUGGESTIONS FOR READING

The principal obstacle the reader will find to further explorations in the plays of Corneille is the scarcity of translations that are both good and accessible. In general, the tone of the original will be caught best in a verse translation, even though some accuracy may be lost. In addition to *Le Cid,* Corneille's best known plays are *Horace* (1640; also translated *Horatius*), *Cinna* (1641), and *Polyeucte* (1642). In hardcover editions, Lacy Lockert's *Chief Plays of Corneille* (Princeton, 1957), and Paul Landis' *Six Plays of Corneille and Racine* (New York, 1931), contain both readable translations and helpful introductions.

The plays of Racine are more readily available in translation than Corneille's. Although *Phédre* (1677) and *Berenice* (1670) are probably his most powerful plays, *Andromaque* (1667), *Britannicus* (1669), and *Iphigenie* (1674) are representative and well worth reading.

Molière's plays are fortunately available in a wide variety of translations, *Tartuffe* (1667), *Le Misanthrope* (1666), *L'Avare* (*The Miser,* 1668), and *Le Bourgeois Gentilhomme* (*The Would-Be Gentleman,* 1671) being especially recommended.

French Classical Drama

Restoration Comedy

When the Stuart monarchy was restored to the throne of England in the person of the Merry Monarch, Charles II, one of his first official acts was to reopen the theaters by giving an exclusive monopoly of all dramatic productions to two acting companies. But it is doubtful whether more than two would have been practical. The Puritan middle class, now a powerful force in the country, disapproved violently of the theater as a breeding place of vice and immorality. And doubtless there was some truth in their accusations. The English court, exiled in France, had acquired a taste for sophisticated French comedy while losing none of its own essential vulgarity. Somewhat dizzy from its own sudden return to power, the courtier society was certainly frivolous, hedonistic, and very much concerned with simply having a good time. The drama that developed out of this context was, almost necessarily, social in its concerns, comic in its form, and extremely narrow in its perception of reality. Indeed, it was much more effectively coterie theater than what had existed before 1642.

Restoration comedy is probably the most difficult type of English drama for the modern reader to understand. Like French classical tragedy, it is concerned with a decidedly limited kind of reality, unfamiliar to most of us. On the stage its formality and grace provide a degree of aesthetic pleasure, but read in a book we can see little more than complicated plots involving one-sided cardboard people speaking a highly artificial and stilted language. But in a very real sense the artificiality of these plays *is* their reality.

All social relationships are, by their nature, to a degree artificial. Countless arbitrary rules and proprieties are necessary to oil the wheels of social intercourse, and many little hypocrisies and dishonesties are not only countenanced but demanded. One of the favorite subjects of comic literature is the completely blunt and honest person, who always says what he thinks and lets his feelings show and who for that very reason is a social outcast. And for a wealthy and sophisticated leisure class, such as that which formed both subject and audience for Restoration comedy, the form of social behavior tends to become an end in itself—an elaborate game with complicated rules in which the cleverest player is the winner. To shift the metaphor a little, Restoration comedy, with its formality and artificiality, its bowing and scraping, its almost geometrical arrangements and rearrangements of personal relationships, resembles nothing so much as an elaborate eighteenth-century dance, like the minuet. Indeed, most of these comedies end with just such a formal dance, which nicely captures the spirit of an artificial world governed by intricate rules and "steps," as well as by a sense of grace and propriety, where individuals may feel passions of love or hate or jealousy but must not, in public, let them show—where everything is subordinate to form.

A second, and related, aspect of Restoration comedy, which modern readers find difficult to accept on its own terms, is its widely denounced licentiousness. The typical reaction is apt to be either the guilty snicker, as at a distinctly off-color joke, or righteous outrage. But while the joke is certainly there—and Restoration society was far from prudish in its attitude toward

sex—the plays are not so much immoral as amoral. The playwrights were not primarily concerned with moral problems as
such; personal morality is a matter of character, and they were
concerned with manners. The society they wrote about was not
necessarily good—it might very possibly be "bad"—but this was
irrelevant; it existed, and it demanded certain forms, obedience to
a clearly defined code. Right and wrong were largely matters not
of what you did but of how you did it—right and wrong ways of
doing things. The problem was not how to improve society but to
live with it—to learn the way of the world.

The Way of the World (1700) was both the title and the theme
of William Congreve's best-known comedy, probably the finest
example of this highly specialized and limited form of drama,
and as representative as any single play could be of both its
virtues and its weaknesses. "The world" of the title is the world of
high society, and "the way" is the ability to maintain the forms it
requires. But while Congreve seems to accept the practical necessity of conforming to society's demands, he does not dance so
blindly to the world's tune that he imagines it the only reality. He
is quite aware that the individual has needs that run counter to
the music, and the friction between personal desires and social
pressure supplies the central conflict of the play.

In Congreve's play, as in much Restoration comedy, success is
to be judged on the basis of two criteria: Has a character the
cleverness and wit to live up to the code established by society,
and can he satisfy society and get what he wants from it and still
"be himself," still retain his identity and individuality? For the
individual who wants the best of both worlds, the pressures are
great and the pitfalls many. The nature of the dangers that beset
his path in threading a way through the social labyrinth is suggested by the structure and characterization of the play.

It is often complained that the plot of *The Way of the World* is
much too complicated, that there are too many intrigues for even
a reasonably attentive person to follow. This is quite true; but the
very intricacy of the plot is a kind of tangible representation of
the complex relationships and obligations that must be either

168 mastered or circumvented in order to walk successfully the way of the world. The basic situation in the play is the classic one of romantic comedy: Mirabell wants to marry Millamant, but to do so must overcome certain obstacles. The principal hurdle is the need for the approval of Mrs. Wishfort, Millamant's aunt and guardian, who has control over her niece's inheritance. We may be put off somewhat by the young lovers' unsentimental concern for money. In a thoroughly romantic play they would elope to Paris and live happily ever after in blissful poverty; but Congreve is realistic enough to recognize that even people in love usually want to remain in the society in which they have been brought up and whose values they accept. The plot, then, consists mainly of Mirabell's efforts to win both Millamant and her fortune.

Just before the play begins Mirabell has made his job harder by completely alienating Mrs. Wishfort. In order to gain access to the niece, he pretended to woo the widowed aunt; but the truth has come out, and Mrs. Wishfort plans to get revenge by marrying Millamant to her nephew, Sir Wilfull, and marrying Mirabell's uncle, Sir Rowland, herself (thus disinheriting the nephew). Mirabell counters with a second plot, this time planning to pass his servant, Waitwell, off as Sir Rowland, and counting on the fact that when Mrs. Wishfort discovers the truth she will grant Millamant and himself anything to be released from such a humiliating marriage (which Mirabell would do by then revealing that Waitwell was already married to Foible and not legally married to Mrs. Wishfort at all). When this plot fails as well, Mirabell is driven to abandon his complicated machinations and masquerades. He first wins Mrs. Wishfort's trust by giving up his claims on Millamant and then, by rescuing her from Fainall's attempted blackmail, gains her undying gratitude for his honesty and foresight.

This summary sounds a great deal simpler than the play. But in fact the play *looks* a great deal more complicated than it *is*; and this in itself is a comment on the way of the world. Much of the intricacy of the action arises from the unsuccessful efforts of the various characters to outwit and outmaneuver each other for a variety of reasons—all of which produces a great deal of sound and fury but no results. Mirabell himself has embarked on several involved projects to win Millamant; but they are all failures, and in the end it is not so much his own plots as the fact that Fainall has overplayed *his* hand that permits Mirabell to step in, prove himself the cleverer, and win all the marbles. The plot itself, in other words, is fairly straightforward, but it is encrusted with endless illustrations of "gamesmanship"—and in the end it is the wisest and cleverest player who wins.

Another element contributes to the seeming complexity of *The Way of the World*. Early in the play, the apparent relationships between the characters are directly opposed to the real ones. Mirabell has been pretending to be in love with Mrs. Wishfort while he is really wooing Millamant; and Millamant pretends to be fashionably indifferent. Mrs. Wishfort, a "superannuated" widow, tries to play the role of a gay young thing looking for a husband. Mr. Fainall is most solicitous about his wife's welfare but is in fact having an affair with Mrs. Marwood, who is really, it comes out, in love with Mirabell. Sir Wilfull has been pushed into the role of Millamant's suitor, although he would much prefer to be drinking with the wenches in the kitchen. And Sir Rowland is only Mirabell's valet. But all these roles and false relationships turn out to be little more than self-deceptions, and by the end of the play they are replaced by something closer to the truth. Mrs. Wishfort sees herself as the foolish old widow she is, Sir Rowland is exposed, Mrs. Fainall sees her husband and her "friend" Mrs. Marwood for what they are, Sir Wilfull leaves to drink in the taverns of Europe, and Mirabell and Millamant declare themselves as lovers, to each other and to the world.

The fact that Congreve takes the trouble to break down the social façade does not mean, however, that the façade is not real. And in such a society, where playing the game and maintaining a role are obviously so important, those who are not clever enough to do the job properly will almost inevitably be the objects of ridicule and satire. Indeed, most of the characters in Restoration comedy can be classified according to that criterion, and *The Way of the World* is no exception. There are, in the first place, those who fail to live up to the ideal either because they are outsiders or because of stupidity. Sir Wilfull Witwoud is not stupid, but he doesn't know the rules. He is baffled by his brother's fatuous formality on his arrival in London, and from then on blunders his way through the play, likable but uncouth, until he is totally demolished in the scene where he is supposed to be making love to Millamant but has not a fine word in his head. Petulant, on the other hand, is a fool. He thinks that being sharp-tongued and critical, taking offense at everything, is the way to be a gallant; but he only succeeds in making himself a standing joke to those cleverer than he.

On the other hand there are those characters who have become so caught up in the gamesmanship and role-playing of society that they seem to be nothing *but* a role—to have no reality behind the mask. The classic example of this kind of figure is in another play, Sir Fopling Flutter in Etherege's *Man of Mode* (1676), who is nothing but a clotheshorse, who can talk or think of nothing but the latest fashion and who has thereby surrendered his manhood to an empty form. In *The Way of the World* we find Witwoud, who is described as a fool "made up of scraps of other people's wit," but who has no personality of his own. More important to the play is Mrs. Wishfort, who takes her role of the "merry widow" seriously and tries to impose it on others. The scene where we first see her (III.i) is almost symbolic in the richness of its implications. We find the old crone sitting among her paints and rouge pots preparing the mask with which she will go out to face the world. At one point her very real emotions literally crack the varnish of her role; but she is assured that it can be repaired to match the picture of her younger self. It is relevant, too, that in this scene she is much concerned that Sir Rowland will make the advances so that she can maintain the "decorums" and proprieties demanded of her by her role.

Finally, there are the successful ones, the Mirabells and Millamants, who learn the way of the world, who master the *art* of 171 living in it and yet can find a way of being themselves—that is, not only adjust to the world but adjust it to *them*.

Characterization in drama is necessarily accomplished through dialogue; but in *The Way of the World* there is an unusually close relationship between the way in which a character uses language and his place in the social pattern Congreve has set up. Taken as a whole, the language is as polished and graceful as the society that Congreve wrote about. But language is also used in a variety of ways in the play and, in fact, like the complexity of the plot, becomes almost a symbol for certain aspects of social relationships.

Witwoud and Petulant, for instance, talk a great deal but rarely say anything. Their chatter is full of clever and generally abusive witticisms but has no purpose. Language for them is not so much communication as simply an opportunity to hear themselves talk —so much hot air to inflate their image of themselves and to impress others with how witty and clever they are. Mrs. Wishfort is a perfect torrent of talk, always silly and generally about herself and her decorums. Language for her is simply a flood of sound, as though to overwhelm or drown out the wishes of the younger people, literally as well as figuratively. Sir Wilfull, naturally, lacks the grace of the others and is as rough and clumsy in his language as he is in his manners. In the specifically social situation, as when he is trying to play the gallant with Millamant, he is totally tongue-tied. In the sense that language is a kind of mask for people like Witwoud and Petulant, Sir Wilfull has no language at all.

Mr. Fainall and Mrs. Marwood are "properly" clever and polished in their talk, but there always seems to be an ulterior motive behind their banter. They use language to probe, to maneuver, to cover up their real motives and to deceive others. Fainall's conversation with Mirabell and Mrs. Marwood's with Mrs. Fainall is full of seemingly friendly chatter, but they are always trying to get something *out* of someone that they can use against him.

It is really only in the persons of Mirabell and Millamant that language becomes something more than a clever and witty disguise or mask, a part of a role, a means of abusing others or of tricking them into revealing secrets. Their talk is as glittering as any in the play, but it is also a means of defining relationships, of seeing themselves and others as they are. Actually, there are only two instances in the whole play when the two lovers are alone together and indulge in the favorite social game of the age, the battle of words—and a comparison of the two episodes is revealing. In the first, early in the play (II.ii), both are still playing their roles, behaving as they are expected to behave: Mirabell playing the solemn, heartsick lover ("You are merry, madam, but I would persuade you for a moment to be serious") and Millamant the silly, flighty flirt ("What, with that face? no, if you keep your countenance, 'tis impossible I should hold mine"). And there is no communication between the two. The second conversation between the lovers is such a key scene that it has been given a name by later critics: the Proviso or Bargaining Scene. It is the long dialogue in Act IV in which Mirabell and Millamant define the terms of their future marriage relationship. The language is that of comic repartee, but it has serious undertones; and while the terms of the "agreement" may seem trivial, they are closely relevant to the theme of the play.

Millamant's conditions, for instance, all reflect a desire not to be forced into the conventional role of a wife:

> I won't be called names after I'm married, ... as wife, spouse, my dear, joy, jewel, love, sweetheart, and the rest of that nauseous cant, in which men and their wives are so fulsomely familiar. . . . Nor shall we go to Hyde-park together the first Sunday in a new chariot, to provoke eyes and whispers, and then never to be seen there together again; as if we were proud of one another the first week, and ashamed of one another ever after.

And Mirabell has his own set of comparable conditions:

> *Item,* I article, that you continue to like your own face, as long as I shall; and while it passes current with me, that you endeavour not to new-coin it. . . .

Concepts of Reality in the Great Periods of Drama

Item, when you shall be breeding . . . I denounce against all
strait lacing, squeezing for a shape, till you mould my boy's
head like a sugar-loaf, and instead of a man child, make me
father to a crooked billet.

There are more items on both sides, but the direction is obvious.
The emphasis on Millamant's part is on the freedom to be herself,
that she may not "dwindle into a wife," and on Mirabell's, on her
promises not to force her nature for the sake of appearances, that
he "may not be beyond measure enlarged into a husband." They
will not be mere roles, but flesh-and-blood human beings.

It is significant that this bargaining scene between Mirabell and
Millamant is sandwiched between two very different proposals,
the clumsy, uncouth wooing of Millamant by the inarticulate Sir
Wilfull and the extravagant, passionate, verbally polished, but
entirely false wooing of Mrs. Wishfort by the ultimate example of
the role-player, the valet Waitwell disguised as Sir Rowland.
These represent the two extremes of blunt incivility and polished
hypocrisy between which Mirabell and Millamant have found a
middle way. They neither turn their backs on society nor surren-
der to the falseness of its masks, but learn to live with it without
losing their identity or each other; and their clear-sighted attitude
toward both it and themselves gives them the only stable relationship in the play.

Because the characterization in *The Way of the World* seems
flat and one-sided, because it employs a polished and consistently
witty language such as no one ever actually spoke, and because
the situations are frankly improbable and contrived, it may be
difficult for us today to see any significant reality behind, or
within, the play. It does not seem concerned with the basic human
dilemmas of *Dr. Faustus,* nor do the follies of human nature represented seem as universal as those in *Twelfth Night.* But although
it may not be a profound play and was certainly written as a
satirical portrait of and for a particular society and therefore had
meaning especially for them, it does concern itself with a kind of
reality that is meaningful to *any* society.

It is possible to say that the essence of civilization lies in finding a compromise between individual impulse and desire and the forms and rules of society. Anyone can follow instinct—animals do it all the time. The problem is to achieve a full life on a natural and emotional and personal level, and still play the game that is the price we pay for being *social* animals. This is the achievement of Mirabell and Millamant and the theme of the play. The comedy, however, as is usual in satire, lies not so much in their success as in the failure of the others. The two lovers are not in themselves comic figures, although there may be comedy in their witty dialogue; but the satire lies in the ridicule of those who fail to find the way of the world, in the best sense.

Congreve's contribution to Restoration drama has received as much attention as it has for several reasons. In the first place, as was suggested earlier, it is representative of a significant shift in focus in English drama—a shift that had really been developing gradually ever since the Middle Ages. Instead of seeing man in terms of an eternal and divinely ordered universe, or of absolute moral law, or even in terms of certain universal elements in human nature, it tends to view man rather narrowly as the representative and product of a specific social context. And English drama ever since the Restoration has found its reality largely in the social relationships and the social values of the contemporary world of its audience.

Of course, the inherent weakness of drama that is social and contemporary is that it will become dated along with the social conditions or problems it treats as being "real." But in some instances a work may, for other reasons, rise above its own particularity and be permanently accepted as a work of art. Restoration comedy at its best—and this includes *The Way of the World*—has achieved just this kind of durability. Congreve, as we have seen, has achieved an almost perfect balance or coalescence among characterization, plot, language, and theme. The witty, sparkling dialogue and the cadenced, graceful speech are not simply pretty decorations but an organic part of the theme and the particular kind of reality of the play. Within its own admittedly limited range, it is a highly polished gem, which can only be matched, if anywhere, in the slightly earlier plays of Molière in France, plays very similar in their perception of "reality." The changes in social conditions will probably always prevent Restoration comedy from being significant or even particularly relevant drama, but *The Way of the World* will always be art.

𝕏𝕏 The Rise of Sentiment and the Fall of Drama

It is one of the paradoxes of dramatic history that *The Way of the World,* in spite of the fact that it mirrored a limited social condition, has been more highly acclaimed by later ages than it was by its own, for the truth is that it was dated by the time it was produced. Unfortunately for Congreve, the graceful and artificial society of the minuet and the masquerade ball, the one he had grown up in and wrote about, no longer dominated his audience when the play appeared in 1700.

"Upper-class" drama, and the sophisticated courtier world to which it addressed itself, had thrived under the Merry Monarch, the witty and profligate Charles II. But Charles died in 1685, his brother James II lasted only three years, and in the "Glorious Revolution" of 1688 Parliament deposed James and put William and Mary on the throne of England. William III was a sour and suspicious Dutchman, not overly fond of the English and much happier on the battlefields of Europe fighting the French than as a leader of high society. But the Glorious Revolution reflected a much more basic change than the personality of the king, for with it came a tremendous increase in the power of Parliament. It had deposed a king and named his successor. Moreover, William's wars in Europe cost money, and Parliament provided it only in return for greater power. And Parliament was dominated by the middle-class merchants and businessmen who were, in effect, financing the country. What was happening was, in fact, the last stage in a process that had begun with the break-up of the feudal system; financial power had passed from the landed aristocracy

The Restoration Through the Nineteenth Century

to the merchant middle class and, with it, political and social power. And however idealistic we may be about art, the theater will follow the money, just as it did when it moved from the popular theater of Shakespeare's day to the private "coterie" theaters of Jacobean London.

So it was that by the time of Congreve's last play middle-class values and tastes controlled the English stage. And the middle class was not particularly interested in grace and wit, nor in the problem of coming to terms with the forms and decorums of high society. They, as a class, had risen through hard work, thrift, and financial shrewdness; and as for Congreve's values of balance and reason, the only balance they were concerned with was in their bank account, and the primary function of reason was to justify the unrestricted acquisition of money. But if the nasty business of making money soured their souls by day, they could in the evening find sweet relief in the escapist world of the theater. And they did not want to be disturbed by the haunting questions of high tragedy or the unsettling barbs of satire. The typical businessman did not want his values and his morality questioned—perhaps they were all too questionable to him. He wanted, rather, to be reassured. No matter how hard-headed he might be on the Board of Trade, he wanted to be reminded that deep down inside he had a heart of gold. And what easier way of proving one's basic good nature than by shedding an honest tear—in the theater—for widows and orphans thrust out in the howling blizzard, or a tear of joy at seeing downtrodden virtue rewarded? What easier way to wash off the dust and guilt of the day than by submerging oneself in the softer and more liquid emotions? And the theater will generally give an audience what it wants. Thus, by the time of *The Way of the World*, theaters were becoming increasingly teary places—and by the middle of the eighteenth century had virtually floated away.

Another factor contributed to the shift in tone and subject matter in drama. With the rise of the middle class came a rise in the influence of Puritanism, the powerful middle-class faction of the Church of England. We are all familiar with the popular

image of the Puritans who had settled in New England a half
century or so before: stern, grim, sour spoil-sports, who never
smiled and spent most of their time in church. This is an obvious
exaggeration; but it is true that the Puritans had always disapproved strongly of the stage as a hotbed and breeding place of
immorality and vice. About Congreve's time, under Puritan influence, several influential pamphlets appeared attacking the theater and propounding the thesis that "the business of plays is to
recommend virtue and discountenance vice." And whatever else
Restoration comedy may have been, or done, it wasn't *that*.

And so, for the middle-class audience after the turn of the
eighteenth century, the values, the problems, the social relationships of Restoration comedy simply did not represent a meaningful reality. And since this audience saw the function of drama
as didactic rather than aesthetic, the grace and balanced form of a
play such as *The Way of the World* was taken as evidence of
decadence rather than of artistic craftsmanship.

What the audience wanted was to be amused ("amuse" literally means "to waste time") under the guise of moral improve-
ment; and the theater offered this group escape in its sentimentality, and self-congratulation in its morality. "Sentimental
Drama" is, in fact, the label given to this misbegotten tradition
that dominated the stage virtually until Wilde and Shaw rescued
comedy at the end of the nineteenth century. It included both
pseudo-tragedy and pseudo-comedy—"pseudo" because the comedy was not comic and the tragedy was only pathetic. The standard ingredients were, as the label implies, a plenitude of tears
and sufficient improbable situations to produce them, involving
the suffering of unrecognized virtue, the separation of parents
and children, misunderstood letters and misplaced jewels—in
other words, endless accidents and mistakes that in comedy were
set right, amid tears of joy, and in tragedy were not. And to all
this was added the spice of explicit and heavy-handed moralizing.

None of this class of plays deserves detailed discussion, but a
few illustrations may be revealing. *The Conscious Lovers* (1722)
by Sir Richard Steele (who with Addison wrote *The Spectator*)

The Restoration Through the Nineteenth Century

announces in its prologue that its purpose is "with breeding to refine the age,/ To chasten wit, and moralize the stage." And in this Steele is depressingly successful. The play is nominally a comedy, but the humor is negligible. There is a great deal of talk about generosity and benevolence, and the principal character is a quite unbelievable paragon of these virtues. In the Preface, Steele explains the sense in which the play is a comedy:

> Anything that has its foundation in happiness and success must be allowed to be the object of comedy; and sure it must be an improvement of it to introduce a joy too exquisite for laughter, that can have no spring but in delight. The tears which were shed [at the performance] flowed from reason and good sense. . . . To be apt to give way to the impressions of humanity is the excellence of a right disposition and the natural working of a well-turned spirit.

The quick-flowing tear at the sentimental situation, then, was tangible evidence of a virtuous and benevolent heart—which is precisely what the audience wanted to hear and why they wanted to cry. The moral of the play, addressed to the hero at the end, was also what the audience wanted to hear:

> You have set the world a fair example. Your happiness is owing to your constancy and merit, and the several difficulties you have struggled with evidently show—
> What e'er the generous mind itself denies,
> The secret care of Providence supplies.

Be generous, he seems to say, because Heaven will see that you get it back with interest; benevolence, in a word, is a good investment!

In the tragic vein is Lillo's *The London Merchant* (1731). The audience to which it is directed is suggested by the title but is even more obvious in the dialogue. The benevolent merchant, Mr. Thorowgood, is lecturing his apprentice Trueman:

> 'Twill be well worth your pains to study trade as a science, to see how it is founded in reason and the nature of things; how it promotes humanity, as it has opened and yet keeps up an intercourse between nations far remote from one another in situa-

tion, customs, and religion; promoting arts, industry, peace and
plenty; by mutual benefits diffusing mutual love from pole to
pole. (III.i)

One can imagine the good burghers, who had been afraid that all
they were doing was making money, glowing with modest pride
at this; and the play, in spite of its obvious crudity, was probably
the most popular play of the eighteenth century. The purpose
which the play was designed to serve is again pointed out in the
concluding lines:

> In vain
> With bleeding hearts and weeping eyes we show
> A human, gen'rous sense of others' woe,
> Unless we mark what drew their ruin on,
> And, by avoiding that—prevent our own. (V.iii)

This is, in itself, a perfectly tenable theory of art; and certainly
benevolence and generosity are not virtues to be sneered at. The
trouble with Sentimental Drama was that it did not do what it
professed. It preached morality loudly enough, but it did not
make it *real* in meaningful dramatic terms. It tended to be superficial in its moral values, tawdry in its emotion-mongering, completely divorced from reality in its characterization and in the
arbitrary contrivance of its plots. It usually represented good and
bad in such black-and-white terms that the audience had no
trouble at all identifying themselves with the virtuous characters
and seeing the rest as "other people." And all this under the pretense of presenting an image of contemporary reality. Sentimental
Drama, in other words, was little more than a form of escapist
melodrama, which soothed the moral sense by flattering the complacency and self-righteousness of the audience. It is, taken as a
whole, a failure as dramatic art because it has little to do with
reality in *any* significant sense, even the literal. And art, as has
been suggested before, is a means of coming to terms with reality,
not of escaping it.

Thus it was that the pernicious influence of didactic morality
and sentimentality, combined with an almost complete disregard
for the necessity of keeping contact with some kind of reality,

rotted the fibers of an art form that, however cynical and amoral it may have been, produced the most brilliant comedies England would see for two centuries. Richard Brinsley Sheridan was almost the only island in a sea of tears.

Sheridan is not the only exception to the exclusive dominance of the sentimental tradition (John Gay and Henry Fielding burlesqued it effectively); but because he, along with Oliver Goldsmith, represents a conscious rebellion against "weeping comedy," his work is perhaps the most important. His plays are also concrete evidence that the glorification of the sentimental virtues, warm-heartedness, generosity, and pity, need not in itself produce bad drama.

Sheridan, like Congreve, was very much a part of the genteel, upper-middle-class audience he wrote about. Like Congreve, he knew its graces and follies at first hand, and he satirized its extravagances while he accepted many of its values. But the values were quite different. The "high society" Sheridan pictures is, in effect, the aggressively moralistic merchant class of Congreve's time who have since bought or married their way into titles and become the idle rich themselves; and the values to which they pretend are not those of the Restoration courtier, but those enshrined in Sentimental Drama. Sheridan was part of this class, even though its pretensions and hypocritical moralizing revolted him.

Sheridan's *School for Scandal* (1777) is one of the most successful and most durable English comedies. It has both the wit and satire of Congreve, and if it lacks the verbal polish and brilliance of *The Way of the World* it also lacks its coldness. For however admirable the sparkling dialogue and pointed wit of Restoration comedy, and even though normal human emotions may exist behind its shining surface, there is something hard and brittle and essentially heartless about it. It appeals primarily to the intellect; but the intellect is not the whole man. Of course Sentimental Comedy was in part trying to supply what was missing in Restoration comedy, but it is more offensive in its excess of emotion than the latter is in its lack of it. Sentimental Comedy disgusts the intellect because it cannot make a valid and honest appeal to the heart; it insists on an emotional response that a thinking person is unwilling to give. And this is the essence of sentimentality: to demand more emotion than the situation justifies.

But Sheridan, although he obviously respects the sentimental virtues of warm-heartedness and benevolence, does not treat them sentimentally. In his plays the situations and even the characters are often typical of Sentimental Comedy, but the *tone* is not. In other words, he includes sentiment or feeling without insisting on it. For example, the scene at the end of *School for Scandal,* when Charles discovers the true identity of his uncle and benefactor Sir Oliver, is a comic discovery rather than the tearful reunion that concludes *The Conscious Lovers.* Again, in one of the central episodes of the play, Charles's auction of the family portraits, the comedy is provided by the refreshing irreverence with which he sells off his stiff and stuffy ancestors to pay for his gay life. And of course the comedy is heightened by our knowledge that "little Premium" is Uncle Oliver in disguise. But the heart of the scene is Charles's refusal, out of sentiment, to sell the "ill-looking little fellow over the settee"—Uncle Oliver's portrait—for any amount of money. Equally important is the sentimental effect of this on the good-hearted uncle, who will now forgive his nephew anything. The whole tone of the episode is sharply anti-sentimental, and yet the implicit values are those professed by Sentimental Comedy.

So too, the episodes which contrast the generosity of Charles, who gladly gives his poor relative "Mr. Stanley" money rather than pay his own creditors, with the empty promises and platitudes of the pious Joseph, are at once satirical and sentimental in the values assumed. Charles himself is a sentimental hero, the scapegrace playboy with the heart of gold; and irresponsible generosity and good nature are about the only virtues that can be claimed for him. And, characteristically, his "reward" at the end of the play is not for his cleverness or self-understanding but for his virtue. But Charles does not exist for the sake if his virtues, as he would in a typical Sentimental Comedy—so that we could weep for joy when he wins the hand of Maria. Charles is present mainly as part of the satire, to show up by contrast his mealy-mouthed sentiment-quoting brother Joseph and the role-playing society of which he is a part. But again, the terms in which the two are contrasted are the goodness of their hearts and the sincerity of their generosity.

Sheridan is defending, not attacking, the virtues of benevolence, charity, and pity that are associated with the Sentimental tradition; and he is defending them against the plays and the people that loudly proclaim these values without in fact possessing them. Joseph Surface in a sense is representative of Sentimental Comedy as Sheridan saw it in the theater of his time, pretending to sentiment and morality and emotions that were essentially false. And it is largely because Sheridan is so concerned with genuineness that he does *not* go over the edge into sentimentality; through sheer good humor and common sense he keeps a perspective other playwrights lacked.

Sheridan's significance, then, lies not only in the fact that he tried to bring laughter back into the theater, but in that he also tried to bring back reality. Sentimental Comedy is false because its characters are as simple-mindedly good or bad as Morality figures set down in a supposedly "real" world, because it presents them with no genuine moral dilemmas, and because it has no steady vision of life except as a kind of emotional gymnasium. But that Sheridan has a view of life is evident in his sharply satirical portrait of contemporary society and social types; his world presents dilemmas in the patent ambiguity of appearance and reality; and while Joseph's piety and sentiments are simply the mask of a self-seeking hypocrite, Charles's virtue is not entirely pure, nor is his generosity beyond the taint of folly. Sheridan, in his view of both morality and human nature, keeps a grasp on reality that most of his contemporary playwrights had lost, and which might have brought English drama back to its senses.

What is most surprising about Sheridan's plays is not so much his success, in spite of going against the current of popular taste,

but that he had so little effect. Comedy continued to be like
Joseph Surface, mouthing easy morality and weeping crocodile
tears, and the same audience that had enjoyed *School for Scandal*
enjoyed the plays ridiculed therein as much as ever. As so often
happens, the satire missed its mark, and the audience laughed
without knowing it laughed at itself. And so, in spite of Sheridan's
valiant efforts to stem the tide of sentimentality and bring laughter and common sense back into the theater, the course of English
drama continued downhill into, and largely through, the nineteenth century.

It is easy to oversimplify the forces that brought English drama
to the lowest point of its history. They are economic, social, cultural, even political—indeed, in many ways the same forces that
had begun the decline at the end of the Restoration period with
the rise of Sentimental Drama. The audience was essentially the
same, the ever-growing middle class, and the theater was increasingly commercial in the worst sense of the term—that is to say,
pandering to the lowest common denominator in the taste of its
audience. And that taste was for much the same thing, the
escapism of emotional stimulation. But the devices that had produced suspense and tears in 1720 had begun to pall by 1820,
and playwrights were forced to dig ever deeper into their bag of
tricks. As a consequence, the characteristic tendency of nineteenth-century drama was toward sensationalism; and sensationalism, depending as it does on novelty, surprise, the incredible
and the forbidden, involves almost by definition a divorce from
anything that can reasonably be called reality.

The sentimental tradition continued on unbroken, but its playwrights had to work harder at improbable pathetic situations to
wring tears from a hardened audience. Laughing comedy reap-
peared, it is true, but it relied largely on the cheap laughs of absurdity and slapstick and in general can only be considered farce
of the most trivial kind. Melodrama was probably the most popular fare, but even it had to rely more and more on stage machinery and special effects—blue fire, exploding castles, Flying
Dutchmen and Specter Bridegrooms. This was the age of the his-

torical "spectacular," such as *The Siege of Gibraltar* mentioned in Chapter Two, stage pieces without plot or characterization, relying on a kind of spurious realism and horrendous effects for their appeal. Shakespeare was so often revived that he has been called the major playwright of the nineteenth century; but again, his plays were exploited for their sensational elements and as spectacular vehicles for the "stars" of the day.

The low estate of the stage produced a kind of vicious circle, and few men of genuine literary talent were willing to prostitute themselves to contemporary tastes. Most of the Romantic poets, it is true—with somewhat snobbish disclaimers about writing for the popular theater—tried their hands at plays. But they were as a group ignorant of both the principles of dramatic art and the practical demands of the theater, and they were too uncompromising to learn. The plays of Byron and Coleridge and Shelley, with their blank verse and their themes of murder, revenge, and incest, sound rather like sensational Jacobean melodrama and seem designed more to bring back the lost glories of the past than to create a new and meaningful drama of the present.

With no serious effort to stem the tide of sensationalism, theaters became increasingly desperate in their efforts to keep their audiences amused. Drury Lane kept a feeble play on the boards by persuading a *real* dog to rescue the heroine nightly from a tank of water. A play entitled *Thalaba the Destroyer* (1836), according to a contemporary review, introduced onto the stage "Burma bulls, elephants, ostriches, and heavens knows what besides from the Surrey Zoological Garden."[1] Further evidence, if such is needed, of the debauchery of public tastes can be found in the fad of the child actors. One William Betty, a thirteen-year-old, achieved two years of notoriety and was followed by some twenty or thirty infant wonders, ranging in age down to seven years: "Infant Columbine," "Young Orpheus," Infant Hercules," and so on, all playing adult roles in supposedly "serious" plays.

[1] Quoted by Allardyce Nicoll in *A History of English Drama, 1660–1900*, IV, 25–26.

And at one point Drury Lane livened things up by including on its bill something called The Human Fly, who walked across the ceiling!

But nineteenth-century drama also had something positive to contribute to the development, and even the reality, of the theater. However bad it may have been, and perhaps because it *was* bad, and had to rely on something besides artistic merit, it placed a premium on the mechanics of play writing and play production. This is, after all, also the age of the Well-Made Play. Skillfully constructed, cleverly cutting the entanglements of the plot in a surprise ending, relying heavily on contrivance and coincidence, these plays still possessed a strong sense of causal relationships that gave them a kind of logical reality. This is also, as we have seen, the period when the mechanical possibilities of the physical stage, under the stimulus of the demands of sensationalism, underwent tremendous expansion and development. And both of these elements were essential before the realistic drama of the twentieth century was possible.

One thing further was necessary, however, and that was a sense that drama was "about" something, was more than an idle entertainment to while away an evening. As a matter of fact, in the middle of the nineteenth century a few practicing playwrights, the best known of whom is Arthur Wing Pinero, sensed the hollowness of contemporary drama and tried to beef it up by introducing a "social problem." The trouble was that too often these problems were only such as could be answered to the complete satisfaction of their middle-class audience. One of their favorites was: Can a fallen woman re-establish herself in polite society and triumph over her past by marrying a gentleman? And the answer, highly gratifying to that self-righteous society, was a resounding No. In other words, what might be called the Well-Made Problem Play raised questions to which everyone had the same answer—and were therefore not really problems at all. It patted its audience on the head and sent it out feeling that it had been correct all along in thinking a gentleman should not marry a woman with a shady background. It is the drama of the *status quo,* of things as they are, of complacency and self-congratulation, much as Sentimental Drama had been, and its social issues were too often only a game.

But in spite of their speciousness as genuine social drama, this group of plays does represent a marked advance over the farces and melodramas that had dominated the stage. It marks a new reaching out for some kind of contact with the reality of human nature and the human situation. It suggests the first stirrings of dissatisfaction with what drama had become, stirrings that would burst abruptly into bloom in the works of Ibsen, Wilde, and Shaw. Pinero may be the last of the Victorians, but he is also the first of the moderns.

SUGGESTIONS FOR READING

Congreve's *The Way of the World* (1700) is probably the best of the Restoration comedies, although *The Man of Mode* (Sir George Etherege, 1676) or *The Plain Dealer* (William Wycherley, 1674) could be used to illustrate the same points.

The Beaux' Stratagem (George Farquhar, 1707) is a good example of a play that lies half way between high Restoration comedy and Sentimental Comedy. The sentimental tradition itself is adequately represented by the plays mentioned in the text. Eighteenth-century plays that rebel against the sentimentality and falseness of the theater are *The Beggar's Opera* (John Gay, 1728), *Tom Thumb* (Henry Fielding, 1730), *She Stoops to Conquer* (Oliver Goldsmith, 1773), *The Rivals* and *The Critic* (Sheridan, 1775 and 1779).

Of the efforts of the Romantic poets to write plays, only Shelley's *The Cenci* (1819) deserves a reading. Other than this, the nineteenth century before Wilde offers little of interest. The best examples of the Well-Made Play are French (*The Glass of Water,* 1840, by Eugene Scribe, or *A Scrap of Paper,* 1861, by Victorien Sardou). The master of the "well-made problem play" was undoubtedly Arthur Wing Pinero (*The Second Mrs. Tanqueray,* 1893, or *The Thunderbolt,* 1910).

An excellent *general* discussion of the whole development of English drama is Alan Downer's *The British Drama* (New York, 1950).

DIRECTIONS AND NON-DIRECTIONS IN MODERN DRAMA 𝔛

A discussion of modern drama ought to begin with some sort of definition of exactly what we mean by the term. Do we refer merely to a set of limiting dates, say 1890 to the present, or are we implying the existence of certain techniques or assumptions that these plays have in common? When we speak of Greek drama or Elizabethan drama or Restoration drama, we refer to groups of plays that in their language, conventions, and thought are largely homogeneous. But the most distinctive feature of modern drama is that it *has* no single distinctive feature. In the past, drama grew organically; each new age built directly on the previous one. There was no conscious effort to rebel, to throw out established traditions. The conventions, symbols, language of the theater were understood and accepted by the audience, and change was slow. But from Ibsen on, the theater has been characterized by multiplicity and confusion.

This diversity in modern drama is, of course, a direct consequence of its origins. When the established traditions of the nineteenth century, the sensationalism of melodrama and the facile triviality of the Well-Made Play, had been discredited by Ibsen and others at the end of the century, what was left was a kind of artistic vacuum. A great service had been done drama in freeing it from a dead tradition; but in a sense a disservice had been done in freeing it from *any* tradition. And there was no shortage of playwrights ready to leap into the breach with theories of what drama should be and do. As a result, there have been almost as many concepts of what kind of reality drama may deal with and how that reality can best be presented as there have been major playwrights.

In one sense, however, there *is* a common element in modern drama, and that too can be traced to its origins. The "New Drama" of the 1890's came into being as a reaction, challenging old ways of doing things as well as old ways of thinking. And the spirit of experimentation in technique and questioning in attitude has remained a characteristic feature of drama, at its best, ever since. The consequence, that it often seems to be heading in a dozen different directions at once, may make any pat generalizations about modern drama difficult but is also evidence of its vitality and excitement.

In the second chapter of this handbook we looked at a few of the plays that illustrate the range of realities dealt with in modern drama. But since the subsequent chapters trace the high points of the development of drama, in terms of its perception of reality, up to the threshold of the modern period, it might be well to continue that approach and reintroduce in a more historical context some of the playwrights mentioned earlier.

By the time of Pinero—thanks to the machinery and scenic effects developed for the melodrama, new advances in lighting, and the introduction of the box, or "fourth wall," set—the English theater had achieved a high degree of visual realism. What was *not* real were the human problems it dealt with or the questions, if any, it asked. Such drama tended, as we have seen, to accept society at its own evaluation of itself. The first important playwright to question seriously the conventional values of his audience was the Norwegian, Henrik Ibsen. His plays, on the whole, deal with the same elements in society as the Well-Made

Play, that is, the professional class and the lesser aristocracy. But his way of dealing with them was very different, and designed primarily to expose the falsity of some of their most cherished beliefs about themselves and their morality. One of his favorite devices was to take a traditionally respected member of the community, a public-spirited businessman, a popular mayor, a respected pastor—men who were, to use the title of one of his early plays, *Pillars of Society*—and show that behind the façade of piety and altruism was a selfishness and unscrupulousness that was all the more vicious because justified in terms of "public good" and "what everybody else does." Mrs. Alving, in *Ghosts* (1881), like many of Ibsen's central characters, is a "learner" in that her eyes are opened to the reality of her previously unquestioned values. Her words, addressed to a typical representative of conventional morality, Parson Manders, could have been spoken by many of Ibsen's heroes and heroines:

> By forcing me to submit to what you called my duty and my obligations; by praising as right and just what my whole soul revolted against, as it would against something abominable. That was what led me to examine your teachings critically. I only wanted to unravel one point in them; but as soon as I had got that unravelled, the whole fabric came to pieces. And then I realized that it was only machine-made.[1]

Ibsen is not critical of morality as such, but of that which has become institutionalized, synthetic, and dead—merely a mask to disguise unrestrained self-interest.

Another favorite device of Ibsen's was to begin his plays where the romantic Well-Made Play ended, with the institution of marriage. The marriage relationship was ideal for his analysis, surrounded as it was by an aura of sanctity and representing the very fountainhead of social morality, and yet hiding behind the doors of the home any amount of deceit, injustice, and brutality. Ibsen delighted in drawing ironic contrasts between what marriage pretended to be and what it was. And what he did to marriage he

[1] *Ghosts*, in *Four Great Plays by Ibsen,* ed. John Gassner (New York: Bantam Books, Inc., 1959), Act II, p. 100.

Directions and Non-Directions in Modern Drama

did, directly or indirectly, to all institutions of "machine-made" morality.

The tradition set in motion by Ibsen of holding a mirror up to society and revealing in realistic terms, not what it wanted to see, but what was *there,* was carried all over Europe: by Zola and Becque in France, by Hauptmann in Germany, by Gorki in Russia, by Galsworthy in England, and by many others. Although it has undergone many small modifications, the same tradition— that of exposing and questioning contemporary social values by recreating on the stage life as it is—can be seen in our own theater: in the angry social drama of the '30's, by men such as Clifford Odets, and more recently in plays such as Tennessee Williams' *Streetcar Named Desire* (1947) and Arthur Miller's *Death of a Salesman* (1949). While social realism is certainly not the only kind of drama to be found on the modern stage, it is probably the most important and durable tradition of the twentieth century.

In England the first substantial rebellion against the banalities of the Well-Made Play did not come until the mid-1890's. This was after translations of some of Ibsen's plays had already appeared, amid violent public denunciation, on the stages of private and experimental theaters. The English reaction, however, when it came, did not take the form of social realism but that of comedy.

It is somewhat ironic that in the perspective of time the serious "problem plays" of men like Pinero have been completely overshadowed by the seemingly empty-headed farce of a flippant young aesthete named Oscar Wilde. Pinero and his fellows at least *tried* to write about real life and real people; but where, in *The Importance of Being Earnest* (1895), is there anything even vaguely resembling reality? Certainly not in its preposterous plot, involving a young man whose only known parent is a black satchel left in the cloakroom of Victoria Station. As for the characters, it is only a question which is the most *im*probable: little Cecily, or the grand dame Lady Bracknell, or the awesome Miss Prism. And not even in the artificial world of Restoration comedy do we find in the dialogue such a steady stream of sparkling witticisms. But the play is *not* empty-headed, and its very im- probability is a kind of pose put on to emphasize its point.

Wilde referred to his play as a "trivial comedy for serious people," implying that it was not one of the serious plays for trivial
people of the contemporary theater. But Wilde's triviality is more
apparent than real; and the genius of *The Importance of Being
Earnest* is that, in spite of its ridiculousness and nonsense, it is
more serious, has more truth and reality in it than the solemn,
realistic problem plays of his day.

The implied inversion of Wilde's comment on his play is characteristic of his method: to turn everything upside down and inside out. He would give his audience the *form* of what was conventional and expected, and then cleverly transmute it into its
opposite. The plot of *The Importance of Being Earnest* is in every
way a conventional one: Boy loves girl, there are parental objec-
tions, the boy proves himself worthy, and boy wins girl. Wilde
goes one better, has two simultaneous romances, and then makes
the situation even more preposterous by having the romantic success of each young man depend not on his personal qualities, such
as sincerity (earnestness), but on his name, Ernest. We also have
the well-worn motif of unknown parentage; but again, the conventional "discovery" scene is reduced to hopeless silliness when
Jack, who only knew that he had been found in a bag in a checkroom, learns that Miss Prism was the one who had left it and
draws the obvious conclusion, embracing that horrified old maid
with the tender cry, "Mother!"

What we have, then, is the typical plot of the romantic Well-
Made Play; but it is a travesty on all Well-Made Plays. All the
familiar gimmicks are there: mistaken identities, improbable dis-
coveries, the mislaid letter (in this case, a mislaid cigarette case),
even mislaid parents. We have the usual characters, too: the "in-
genue" (who wants desperately to meet a wicked man) being
kept in the country to protect her innocence; the bastion of respectable society, Lady Bracknell, who wants to insure a proper marriage for her daughter (she is glad Jack smokes, because "a man
should always have an occupation of some kind"); or the good

Directions and Non-Directions in Modern Drama

country parson (whose sermon on the manna from heaven "can be adapted to almost any situation, joyful, or . . . distressing"). Almost all the clichés of the Well-Made Play are here, but reduced to utter absurdity. In other words, Wilde takes the image of the world and human nature as seen on the contemporary stage, and reveals comically its total divorce from reality.

But Wilde is doing more than exposing the mechanical plots and shallow characterizations of the Well-Made Play to ridicule; he is also showing up the conventionality, the smugness, above all the falsity of its *ideas*. Ideas are normally expressed in language, and it is in the language that lies the real substance, and genius, of *The Importance of Being Earnest*. Much of the humor in the play is verbal and depends on a single basic trick. Wilde employs many variations on the device, but the characteristic pattern is to take a well-known saying and turn it upside down. We are all familiar with the old chestnut about marriages being made in heaven; but it comes out of Algy's mouth: "Divorces are made in Heaven." Or there is the old cliché about lovers: "Two's company, three's a crowd"; Wilde gives it a cynical twist: "In married life, three is company, and two is none." And so, in the course of the play, every cliché, every pompous platitude that provided the moral tone of the Well-Made Plays is turned inside out. The humor of this sort of thing is partly in the shock of surprise, and the pleasure we have in seeing pomposity and pretension deflated. But there is more than this. These inversions of conventional sayings are usually much closer to what people really think than the original sentiments.

Take, for example, Cecily's response to Algy's indignant assertion that he is not wicked: "If you are not, then you have certainly been deceiving us all in a very inexcusable manner. I hope you have not been leading a double life, pretending to be wicked and being really good all the time. That would be hypocrisy." She is using 'hypocrisy' in the opposite of its conventional sense, and therefore saying the opposite of what a sweet and innocent girl would say in a typical romantic play; but most girls in her position would probably rather meet a handsome wicked man than a very good one! Again, in a representative contemporary play Lady Bracknell would be a dignified matriarch staunchly upholding the old way of life and aristocratic values; but in her catechism of Jack in Act I we can see what these values become in Wilde's hands. The implication is, of course, that the social values implicit in the Well-Made Play are in reality just as fatuous and silly as Lady Bracknell's.

But Wilde's wit is aimed not only at the hollowness of the Well-Made Play tradition; he is also challenging fine-sounding but dead ideas that people accept uncritically whether on the stage or in real life. True, he is rarely profound, and he never explores the implications of his witticisms very far. But this, for him, was sufficient. Their *form* is the only comment Wilde intends, and that is enough to serve his purpose of jolting us into taking a second look at the platitudes and worn-out ideas on which we build our image of the world. If Ibsen reveals the reality of contemporary society by tearing off its mask of pretense and showing it as it is, Wilde exposes its falsity, both on and off the stage, by exaggerating it to a ridiculous level of *un*reality. And so, in a sense, we have realism and its direct opposite being used for much the same purpose.

If, in our imaginations, we were to take one part of Ibsen's social conscience and one part of Wilde's wit and fondness for paradox, and leave one part for complete originality, we would come up with a reasonable facsimile of George Bernard Shaw. Shaw's early work was undoubtedly influenced by his admiration of Ibsen, and its staging was entirely within the realistic tradition, but he could never restrain his tendency to see the comic side of human pretension and pomposity, and his characters are often, like Wilde's, more caricatures than Ibsen's psychologically complex figures. Shaw frequently employs Ibsen's favorite device of taking a conventionally respected member of the community and revealing the falsity of his position and the essential dishonesty of his values. In two early plays, *Widowers' Houses* (1892) and

Mrs. Warren's Profession (1905), we are introduced to two obvious representatives of social evil, a slum landlord and the proprietress of a chain of brothels. They are snubbed and scorned by the respectable members of society—until we discover that they are at least a great deal more honest about their source of income than the "pillars of society," whose wealth comes from the same or worse sources.

Shaw also has a penchant for Wilde's characteristic trick of turning conventional platitudes and trite plot situations upside down. *Arms and the Man* (1894) might be called his version of *The Importance of Being Earnest,* for it is also a dramatic spoof of the "romantic comedy view of life," exposing to ridicule a set of values that sees war as noble and glorious, and love as all hearts and cupids—a kind of Valentine's Day pose. There is this difference, however, that the realistic point of view, in the person of Bluntschli, appears *within* the context of the play. The range of Shaw's genius, in both subject matter and technique, is broader than that of either Ibsen or Wilde, but in these and in his later plays his purpose is essentially the same: to force his audience to take a second and more critical look at the ideas and values they have heard so often and have taken for granted.

Shaw differs, moreover, from both Ibsen and Wilde in his concern for ideas as such. For him, reality lies not in the physical world, which is in a constant state of flux, nor in some system of morality, which can also grow old and die, nor in society, which is inherently blind to truth; reality is rather a state of mind, a way of looking at things. In *Man and Superman* (1905), Act III is a kind of philosophical fantasy taking place in Hell. But Heaven and Hell, in the Shavian world, are only parables, and "a parable must not be taken literally. The gulf is the difference between the angelic and diabolic temperament," and "the frontier is only the difference between two ways of looking at things. Any road will take you across it if you really want to get there." And what are these two ways of looking at things? Don Juan, Shaw's mouthpiece, explains that "hell is the home of the unreal and of the

seekers for happiness. It is the only refuge from heaven, which is
. . . the home of the masters of reality." When the Devil asks Juan
what is the use of thinking, the latter answers:

> Why, to be able to choose the line of greatest advantage instead
> of yielding in the direction of the least resistance. Does a ship
> sail to its destination no better than a log drifts nowhither? The
> philosopher is Nature's pilot. And there you have our difference:
> to be in hell is to drift: to be in heaven is to steer.

Reality for Shaw, in other words, is not so much an entity as a
process, a way of seeing the world without the blinders of romance
or self-interest or dead moralities. It is a function of the mind,
not the senses; it does not distinguish black from white so much
as less true ideas from those that are more true. In almost all
Shaw's plays the conflict is between ideas, one that is conventionally accepted and one that is unpopular, but truer; and the characteristic plot pattern carries a character from a situation where
he or she is governed by an illusion, based on conventional ideas
and standards, through a period of disillusionment, and hence to
a new and more clear-sighted perception of reality. And since
reality is a function of the intellect, Shaw's comedy is intellectual,
both in its emphasis on ideas as such and in the wit, paradox, and
satire with which he would stir up the minds of his audience.

Shaw, then, is in his own way as much an iconoclast as Ibsen,
although his method might be described as intellectual rather
than visual realism; and in its own way the Shavian tradition is
almost as important in the contemporary theater as is Ibsen's.
Plays of ideas, not necessarily comedies but always witty and intellectually stimulating, have achieved considerable success in
recent years, most of them (we might note well) coming from
France. Giraudoux's *The Trojan War Will Not Take Place*
(1935; also called *Tiger at the Gates*), Anouilh's *Antigone*
(1944) and *Becket* (1959), Sartre's *The Flies* (1943), and Robert Bolt's *A Man For All Seasons* (1960) all possess a distinctly
Shavian perspective of reality, not in their specific ideas but in
their point of view.

Directions and Non-Directions in Modern Drama

198   There is another and very different sense in which reality can be seen as a function of the mind. Reality may lie not so much in the external world, whether of men or of ideas, as in the subjective or subconscious level of each individual. It was the awareness that there was more to reality than was dreamt of in the philosophy of the social realists that led Strindberg and others to experiment with that projection of subconscious states onto the stage which we call expressionism. Strindberg's symbolic representation of a subjective perception of reality has already been discussed in Chapter Two. It needs to be emphasized, however, that while Strindberg's vision in plays like *The Ghost Sonata* (1907) or *The Dream Play* (1902) is a personal and private one, the *kind* of reality he strives to represent is not. What he and other expressionists are trying to bring out and make dramatically viable is the reality of man's essential, inner, spiritual nature—something that lies behind and beyond his physical existence or even his mind.

We can derive some clues as to the kind of reality sought by the expressionist in the words with which Eugene O'Neill, Strindberg's greatest recent disciple, describes some of his own experiments in expressionism. *The Hairy Ape* (1922), he said, "was propaganda in the sense that it was a symbol of man, who has lost his old harmony with nature, the harmony which he used to have as an animal and has not yet acquired in a spiritual way. . . . And the symbol makes the play either important or just another play." The mask device employed in *The Great God Brown* (1926) he believed "to be the freest solution of the modern dramatist's problem as to how . . . he can express those profound hidden conflicts of the mind which the probings of psychology continue to disclose to us." And *Dynamo* (1929) he called "a symbolic . . . biography of what is happening in a large section of the American (and not only American) soul right now. It . . . will dig at the roots of the sickness of today as I feel it—the death of an old God and the failure of science and materialism to give any satisfying new one for the surviving primitive religious instinct

Expressionism, then, might be called a method of exploring the state of the soul. But it is a technique as much as a perception of reality, and as such it has often been used in plays that in their basic concerns or concept of reality are not in themselves expressionistic. Miller's *Death of a Salesman* (1949), although basically in the tradition of Ibsenian social realism, employs expressionism in its "memory" scenes, as does Williams' *Glass Menagerie* (1944) in its whole "memory play" technique. Indeed, in one form or another expressionism represents one of the favorite devices of the nonrealistic, experimental playwrights.

Another class of plays deserving attention is the loosely defined category known as the Theatre of the Absurd, represented by such playwrights of Eugene Ionesco, Jean Gênet, Samuel Beckett, Harold Pinter, and Edward Albee. The works of these men have gained recognition only in the years since World War II, and most of them vehemently deny that they are part of any self-conscious movement or "school" of drama. Nevertheless, we may well be in the fortunate position of watching a full-fledged dramatic tradition develop before our eyes.

If terms like *modern* and *avant-garde* have any meaning left, they can be applied to the Theatre of the Absurd; but just as in most human affairs there is little wholly new under the sun, so this movement owes much to traditions of the past. Indeed, the very qualities that often lead the casual reader to brand this class of plays as unnecessarily difficult and obscure are those that identify it with the simplest and most elemental of dramatic traditions. The trouble is that we are so accustomed to looking for a paraphrasable "meaning" in our literature that we are apt to search for esoteric meanings in works where no meaning, in our sense, is intended. Martin Esslin, in his valuable book *The Theatre of the Absurd,* tells of the enthusiastic and intelligent re-

[2] Quoted by Barrett Clark, in *Eugene O'Neill, the Man and His Plays* (New York: Dover Publications, 1947), pp. 84, 103–104, 120.

sponse accorded a performance of Beckett's *Waiting for Godot* (1953) by the inmates of San Quentin prison, while the same play had left the more sophisticated critics and audiences of New York and Paris puzzled and annoyed.[3] The point is not that an audience of convicts is necessarily more perceptive than one made up of seasoned playgoers, but that their response was unobstructed by an irrelevant expectation of a clearly defined pattern of meaning.

The tradition of nonsense is at least as old as, and possibly older than, the literature of sense. The nonsensical patter and wordplay and farcical slapstick of Aristophanes' comedies hark back to the Dionysian celebrations of the irrational, which were just as much expressions of a basic human impulse as the more solemn rituals that gave birth to tragedy. The notion that the fool or madman perceives a truth beyond what the world calls wisdom is an old and not primarily literary one, although it has many literary manifestations—the wise fools of Shakespeare or little Pip in *Moby-Dick* being perhaps the most familiar examples. The festivals of topsy-turvy, the Roman Saturnalia, All Fools' Day, Mardi Gras, with their Lords of Misrule, are all expressions of a deep-seated awareness of the element of irrationality and absurdity in the universe, as well as being temporary acts of release from the tyranny of law and logic.

In our own highly organized and efficient world, circumscribed on the one hand by the necessary laws of economics and science and on the other by the idealistic laws of the greatest good for the greatest number, the tradition of nonsense has particular appeal and value. The appeal lies both in the curious exhilaration created by the illusion of freedom from the bonds of logic and morality and in the tacit recognition that there is much in human experience for which reason and logic are inadequate. The value of nonsense lies in the psychological satisfaction we feel when an inner image of the world is given external corroboration, and

[3] Martin Esslin, *The Theatre of the Absurd* (New York: Doubleday & Company, Inc., Anchor Books, 1961), pp. xi-xxiv. My debt to Mr. Esslin will, I suspect, become obvious to anyone who reads this excellent study.

Concepts of Reality in the Great Periods of Drama

in the new angle of vision—or perhaps it is double vision—denied
to reason alone.

The genius of good nonsense lies, of course, not in a total divorce from the familiar world of reason but in the degree to which
it can take the forms and appearance of logic or morality and
exploit some inner inconsistency or absurdity. Lewis Carroll's
nonsense worlds of Wonderland and Looking-glass Country have
a consistent logic of their own; and while it is not the logic of the
"real" world, it throws a healthily disenchanting light on the
tyranny of reason and of language. So too the patter of the old
vaudeville comic team depended for much of its humor on the
incongruous violence done to the "normal" or expected pattern
of logic and grammar. The vaudeville comedian looks backward
to the tradition of the improvised comic dialogue of the Renaissance Italian *commedia dell'arte* and forward to the ribald nonsense, both verbal and nonverbal, of such teams as the Marx
Brothers, or the wild and often strangely moving nonsense of
Charlie Chaplin. On a more sophisticated literary level, Oscar
Wilde's *Importance of Being Earnest* belongs to the nonsense
tradition; for, as we have seen, his basic technique is to reduce
conventional patterns of thought and language to the level of the
absurd.

Since the one element that identifies the Theatre of the Absurd
is, as the label suggests, the representation or at least assumption
of an inherently absurd universe, it is not surprising that it should
rely heavily on the techniques of the nonsense tradition. The context of the plays is a nonsense world, either frankly fantastic or
having that curious nightmare quality where things *look* like
reality but where cause and effect do not operate in a rationally
intelligible fashion and language seems divorced from meaning.
Characteristically, the dialogue of these plays is sprinkled with
verbal play, non sequiturs, puns, nonsense patter, or simply language that has no rational congruity with what is happening.
Similarly, the action frequently reveals an obvious debt to the
non-verbal nonsense tradition of the mime and clown, where theatrical effect is achieved through the use of gesture, action, and

Directions and Non-Directions in Modern Drama

grotesque or incongruous props. And it is no accident that the two most popularly successful productions in the Theatre of the Absurd tradition, Beckett's *Waiting for Godot* and Ionesco's *Rhinoceros* (1959), made use of the talents of two great clowns of the modern stage, Bert Lahr and Zero Mostel.

The Theatre of the Absurd, in other words, makes extensive use of slapstick, both verbal and physical, and it is as futile to seek a complex rational meaning here as it would be in a circus. There is, however, this difference: that the absurdity of the clown or the Saturnalia, while it recognizes the irrational element in experience, is designed as a temporary release from the oppressive fetters of rationality. We know better; we tell our children that seventeen clowns won't "really" fit in a tiny car, and after the Mardi Gras comes repentance and reformation. But in the Theatre of the Absurd we are asked to contemplate a condition of existence from which there is *no* escape.

Although in its techniques the Theatre of the Absurd borrows heavily from an ancient and honorable stage tradition, philosophically it is much more modern. While the theater of the past has recognized the reality of the absurd, it has usually had some order, if not of reason at least of divine law, to fall back on. But the playwrights of the Absurd have no such assurance. They owe something, perhaps, to Pirandello's explorations of "reality" and his *reductio ad absurdum* of all oversimplified conceptions of it in *Six Characters in Search of an Author*. The most direct intellectual debt, however, is to the existentialism of Sartre and Camus, with its image of man set arbitrarily in an absurd and meaningless universe. In this view of the universe, isolation and absolute uniqueness are necessary conditions of existence and, when recognized, engender a fear approaching horror both at the aloneness and at the responsibility implied. Morality, in such a world, is self-created, and values are a function of behavior rather than the other way around. All the conventional abstractions—of traditional morality, of logic, of language—because created by "others," have no validity, and when we behave as though they

Concepts of Reality in the Great Periods of Drama

did, we are comical and nonsensical. Most of the plays of the Theatre of the Absurd seem based on the general assumptions of existentialism, but it is significant that the playwrights do not necessarily consider themselves formal existentialists nor is their work designed to set forth a philosophical principle in the sense that Sartre's *Flies* is. They are, as a group, trying to represent a condition rather than state an idea.

For this reason, the greatest debt of all, at least within the realm of drama, is to Strindberg and the expressionistic playwrights who followed him. Expressionism, characteristically, represents not so much an action as a state of mind; and, as was the case in Strindberg's *Ghost Sonata* and *Dream Play,* the state of mind that is the object of "imitation" in the Theatre of the Absurd represents in turn the playwright's vision of the human condition. Since this kind of drama is concerned with a state rather than an action, it tends to be static or what might be called nonlinear, in the sense that traditional drama moves in a line, which we call plot, from point A to a point B that is different. The dynamic element, then, lies not in the conflict of forces or values, the development of character, or a change in situation, so much as in the process of revelation—or, to describe it from the observer's point of view, the process of discovery. The climax comes not as a function of the action, the resolution of a dilemma or the overcoming of an obstacle, but as the final overwhelming brushstroke in a painting of the human condition.

But the painting, when it is done, is as nonrepresentational as anything by Picasso or Klee. The Theatre of the Absurd is nonrational both in the sense that the universe it postulates is irrational and meaningless and in its method, which is not designed to appeal primarily to the mind, either through logical argumentation (as in Shaw) or through a convincing representation of reality in *some* sense (as, say, in either Ibsen or Shakespeare). The world it offers us is frankly the ephemeral fantasy of the playwright's mind, and its claim to authority is simply that in its absurdity it is more real than the structured and more or less reasonable world we pathetically hope is "reality." And it is the *sense* of absurdity that these plays strive to establish, rather than the metaphysical fact.

Because of this distrust of reason, the Theatre of the Absurd also tends to de-emphasize the role of language, which, especially in its use of abstractions, can impose a specious pattern and logic on things that do not in fact possess them. Debauched by political aspirants, by Madison Avenue, by intellectual dilettantes, as well as by all who parrot them, language has become inadequate to deal with the kind of reality the Theatre of the Absurd seeks to suggest. And so, characteristically, the plays either rely heavily on the visual and gestural or fall back on the hollow clichés of everyday speech whose insufficiency is painfully obvious. Language in the plays frequently becomes a medium of *non*-communication—and this is precisely the point intended.

It may seem incongruous to speak of such plays as having a purpose, but they do, and it is one not far removed from the Aristotelian definition of the purpose of tragedy. By confronting explicitly and imaginatively the mystery and irrationality and absurdity of the human condition, they perhaps offer a kind of catharsis for the horror and self-pity these conditions produce in our subconscious, if not in our conscious, minds.

But whatever else it may or may not be, the Theatre of the Absurd is thoroughly modern. It is modern because it is trying to deal in contemporary terms, and in a language meaningful to the twentieth century, with some of the traditional concerns of drama. It is unquestionably experimental in its methods; and it is constantly challenging and questioning conventional, "machine-made" values. It is rebelling against all that it takes to be dead and petrified, whether in religious or social thought, and against the inadequacy of language and logic to touch reality at all. It is, in many respects, anti-literary, even anti-dramatic; but it is certainly ultra-theatrical. It is often intellectually repulsive while being—and the paradox is quite intentional—emotionally effective.

At a point, however, it becomes a little ridiculous to talk about

realism, expressionism, drama of ideas, and possibly the Theatre
of the Absurd, there exist fairly substantial bodies of work—substantial at least in quality—that establish the identity of a tradition. But a vast number of major playwrights, or plays, are be-
twixt and between; they do not clearly belong to *any* of the major
traditions, and in a sense they constitute a tradition of one. Pirandello's plays have something in common with the Shavian drama
of ideas, but they are much more metaphysical and much less
concerned with social and practical issues. Sean O'Casey began
as a social realist—but the society he would expose is very different from Ibsen's. Bertolt Brecht, a major force in the modern
theater, requires a category all his own. In the end we may have
to accept the somewhat unsatisfactory view that there are almost
as many traditions, and perceptions of reality, as there are playwrights. And this, to come back where we started, is both what
is right and what is wrong with modern drama.

O'Neill, at the beginning of his "experimental period," said
that he was "trying to create a new language for the theatre." And
so are most of the major dramatists of the twentieth century, with
the result that there are a dozen languages of the theater, and
most of them must be learned as part of the experience of the
play itself. This is confusing to the average playgoer or play reader.
If we joined a book club only to find that we were sent books in
Russian and Arabic and Chinese as well as English, unless we
were linguists we would soon turn in our card and join another
club. And so the potential playgoer waits until a neighbor or a
reviewer tells him that a play is in English—or goes to the movies.
The effect has been to create a gap between the popular drama of
Broadway or the movies—too often no more than easily understood amusement—and what might be called "literary" drama,
experimental and exciting but often esoteric and difficult. In
America at least, the split has been intensified by the "hit psychology" of Broadway, which for better or worse is the heart of the
American theater. The economics of Broadway are such that a
play must be a "hit" or nothing; and what makes a hit is a mystery,

206 but it seems to have little to do with artistic or dramatic merit. Once the process starts, the effect is cumulative. The New York theater is heavily supported by tourists and business clients—and the tourist wants to go home with a "hit" to his credit, whatever it is, and the business executive is not going to take a touchy client to a play that may puzzle or upset him.

Thus modern drama, in this country, has been moving in two divergent directions, each carrying its own audience with it; one in danger of becoming as trivial, as vapid, as surely mere amusement as the mid-nineteenth century English theater, the other challenging and vital and in danger of becoming unintelligible. Is this really so bad? "Each to his own taste" seems a reasonable and broad-minded point of view. The truly great drama of the past, however, has never been written for a particular *part* of the total available audience. In ancient Greece, in Elizabethan England, in Europe at the turn of the present century, and to a certain extent today, drama has been intended for everyone, rich and not-so-rich, aristocrat and common man, "egghead" and lowbrow. And I would venture to say that great drama will only be written for the whole of society.

How, then, can the gap be closed? Since the theater is inevitably governed by economics, this will happen only when the "Broadway public," the popular audience, demands more substance in its nourishment, a more meaningful vision of reality. And perhaps this can come about only when, on the one hand, the audience is willing to make some effort to learn the "languages" of the modern theater and, on the other, the experimental dramatist can be persuaded that it is profitable to climb down off Parnassus and speak to the "average playgoer."

This is not to say that such a happy fusion has never occurred. Arthur Miller and Tennessee Williams, who are essentially popular playwrights, have written very substantial plays. And Eugene Ionesco and the American Edward Albee, both identified with the Theatre of the Absurd, have achieved success on Broadway with *Rhinoceros* and *Who's Afraid of Virginia Woolf* (1962),

Concepts of Reality in the Great Periods of Drama

respectively. These are exceptions rather than the rule, but they are encouraging signs.

It should be emphasized, however, that the need is for popular drama to become not less entertaining but *more* entertaining and less an amusement (remembering that to entertain means, literally, "to hold in tension," and to amuse means "to waste time"). Nor is it disturbing that comedy seems to be the staple form of the modern theater. Comedy has sometimes been the medium for escapist theater, and perhaps the constant sense of impending tragedy in the modern world has driven us more and more to look to drama as a relief from reality. But, as has been said before—and it is worth repeating—the world of escape can reflect back on and enlarge our understanding of the world we escape from. In any case, comedy is also an effective medium for the *questioning* that is characteristic of modern theater at its best.

More interesting, though, is what has happened to tragedy in the modern theater. Tragedy also raises questions, and traditionally more basic ones than comedy. Possibly, as far as the commercial theater is concerned, because it *does* ask questions, does demand thought, is disturbing, tragedy lacks the popular appeal to be a money-maker. Even so, tragedy has always been considered the highest form of dramatic art, and one would expect it to attract adventuresome and aspiring playwrights, if only because of its challenge. In some instances it has, but only rarely. Serious (that is, noncomic) drama has tended either to be tragicomic in form or, if the ending *is* "unhappy," as in Shaw's *St. Joan* or Anouilh's *Becket,* to keep the tone light and witty, to shy away from tragedy as something too ponderous and awesome to be attempted. And even where tragedy has been seriously attempted, there is a feeling that somehow it lacks the depth and force of tragedy of the past.

If this is true, the reason probably lies in the kind of reality modern tragedy tends to treat. Certainly realistic social tragedy has suffered from the example of Ibsen. Unlike the Greeks and Shakespeare, who were concerned with man in his eternal and universal aspects, Ibsen was interested in specific social and socio-logical problems and tried to point out specific flaws *in* society. In other words, he wrote "problem plays"—and however real the problems, this was not tragedy, which traditionally has simply *observed* rather than passed judgment on the human condition.

It has sometimes been claimed that Arthur Miller's *Death of a Salesman* comes as close to legitimate tragedy as is possible on the modern stage. Those who object to this view point out that Willy is not adequate as a tragic hero. He is not, in Aristotle's terms, of more than ordinary stature, nor does he achieve any real self-awareness. But these are not the problems; and the appeal to Aristotle is mistaken, because in a way every age has to find its own source of the tragic experience. It can be argued that Willy's very commonness gives him the stature of universality. His fall, like that of Shakespeare's Antony, "is not a single doom . . . and in his name lies a moiety of the world." And there is in Willy's failure the pathos, the sense of essential goodness lost through a tragic flaw, that *is* characteristic of tragedy in the past. Moreover, certain other plays of the modern theater seem in every sense to be tragedies and yet differ from traditional tragedy in just the same respect, plays such as Synge's *Riders to the Sea* (1904), Lorca's *House of Bernarda Alba* (written, 1936; produced, 1945), possibly O'Neill's *Long Day's Journey Into Night* (completed, 1941; produced, 1956).

If *Death of a Salesman* falls short of tragedy at its best, it is for quite another reason—and a reason why most tragedy since Ibsen has failed. At the end of the play, Linda says that she does not understand why Willy has done what he did. But Miller knows, and we know. There is no mystery here; Willy can be fully explained as the product of certain psychological and socio-logical forces. But tragedy contemplates the aspects of human nature and experience that can *not* be explained, that are part of the darkness and mystery and paradox that it is man's glory and tragedy to confront with dignity as well as fear. Williams, like Ibsen, "knows all the answers"; but tragedy acknowledges the

while at the same time reassuring us that behind the apparent contradictions and incoherence there is both dignity and meaning to
existence. Few twentieth-century efforts at tragedy achieve this
dual awareness, possibly because they are tied too closely
to a sociological and scientific concept of reality. But even science
will admit that, after all, the ultimate reality may *be* mystery.

We must be careful, however, not to judge the theater of the
present too harshly because it is not the theater of the past. If
modern drama seems to suffer from the limitations of uncertainty
and confusion, these very elements can also be described as the
virtues of vitality, experimentation, and range of vision. If the
plays of today seem to lack a sense of direction, the apparent
failing may only be the result of our lack of perspective. If our
drama, taken as a whole, seems to have no clearly defined notion
of the kind of reality it is going to treat, this may simply reflect
an awareness that "reality" is a complex and many-sided thing.
And if, in spite of theatrical vitality, we have not yet produced a
Shakespeare, we can take hope by remembering that the early
Elizabethan period was marked by much the same confusion and
variety, both of techniques and of visions of reality, that we see
today. Our responsibility, as playgoers and play readers, is to
understand our playwrights in terms of their own concepts of
what is real, and to encourage in every way we can the best
there is.

SUGGESTIONS FOR READING

Most of the available plays relevant to the discussion in this
chapter either are mentioned in the text or are listed in the reading list appended to Chapter Two. The reader may wish, however, to explore further the field of nonrealistic experimental
drama. For him the following suggestions are offered.

Directions and Non-Directions in Modern Drama

August Strindberg: *To Damascus* (Pts. I and II, 1898; Pt. III, 1940), *The Ghost Sonata* (1907), *A Dream Play* (1902), *There Are Crimes and Crimes* (1899).

Maurice Maeterlinck: *The Intruder* (1890).

Luigi Pirandello: *Henry IV* (1922), *Each in His Way* (1924).

Eugene O'Neill: *The Great God Brown* (1926), *Mourning Becomes Electra* (1931), *Dynamo* (1929), *Days Without End* (1934).

Theatre of the Absurd

Samuel Beckett: *Waiting for Godot* (1953), *Endgame* (1957).

Eugene Ionesco: *The Chairs* (1952), *The Bald Soprano* (1950), *Rhinoceros* (1959).

Jean Gênet: *The Blacks* (1959), *The Balcony* (1957).

Edward Albee: *Who's Afraid of Virginia Woolf?* (1962), *The Zoo Story* (1958), *The American Dream* (1961).

Harold Pinter: *The Caretaker* (1960).

BIBLIOGRAPHY

The following is a selection of titles that may be of interest to the general reader. The list is by no means exhaustive and is offered here in the hope that the reader may wish to explore further either historical or theoretical questions raised by this handbook.

Anthologies which include valuable critical analyses of the plays as well as discussions of the nature of drama:

Brooks, Cleanth, and Robert Heilman. *Understanding Drama.* New York: Holt, Rinehart & Winston, Inc., 1960.

Cubeta, Paul M. *Modern Drama for Analysis.* 3rd ed. New York: Holt, Rinehart & Winston, Inc., 1962.

Downer, Alan. *The Art of the Play.* New York: Holt, Rinehart & Winston, Inc., 1955.

Roby, R. C., and Barry Ulanov. *Introduction to Drama.* New York: McGraw-Hill Book Company, Inc., 1962.

Walley, Harold. *The Book of the Play.* New York: Charles Scribner's Sons, 1950.

212   More general discussions, historical and critical:

Bentley, Eric. *The Life of the Drama*. New York: Atheneum Publishers, 1964.

———. *The Playwright as Thinker*. New York: Meridian Books, 1955.

Clark, Barrett. *European Theories of the Drama*. New York: Crown Publishers, 1947.

Downer, Alan. *The British Drama*. New York: Appleton-Century-Crofts, Inc., 1950.

———. *Fifty Years of American Drama, 1900–1950*. Chicago: H. Regnery Co., 1951.

Esslin, Martin. *The Theatre of the Absurd*. Anchor Books. New York: Doubleday & Company, Inc., 1961.

Fergusson, Francis. *The Idea of the Theatre*. Princeton: Princeton University Press, 1949.

Gassner, John. *Masters of the Drama*. New York: Dover Publications, 1954.

———. *Form and Idea in Modern Theatre*. New York: Holt, Rinehart & Winston, Inc., 1956.

Krutch, Joseph Wood. *The American Drama Since 1918*. New York: George Braziller, 1957.

Steiner, George. *The Death of Tragedy*. New York: Hill & Wang, Inc., 1961.—See especially essays on Corneille and Racine.

Stuart, Donald Clive. *The Development of Dramatic Art*. New York: Peter Smith, 1960.

Styan, J. L. *The Elements of Drama*. Cambridge: Cambridge University Press, 1963.

Weales, Gerald. *American Drama Since World War II*. New York: Harcourt, Brace & World, Inc., 1962.

Collections of provocative essays on various aspects of drama:

Barnet, Sylvan, Morton Berman, and William Burto, eds. *Aspects of the Drama*. Boston: Little, Brown & Co., 1962.

Bogard, Travis, and William I. Oliver, eds. *Modern Drama:*

Essays in Criticism. Galaxy Books. New York: Oxford University Press, Inc., 1965.

Corrigan, Robert, and James Rosenberg, eds. *The Context and Craft of Drama.* San Francisco: Chandler Publishing Co., 1964.

Michel, Laurence, and Richard Sewall, eds. *Tragedy: Modern Essays in Criticism.* Englewood Cliffs: Prentice-Hall, Inc., 1963.

INDEX TO PLAYS

* Indicates a play that is discussed in considerable detail.

Index

39-101